$\mathscr{P}$ROFILES IN WORLD HISTORY

Significant Events and the People Who Shaped Them

P9-CRX-923

(inside back *cover*)

PROFILES IN
WORLD HISTORY

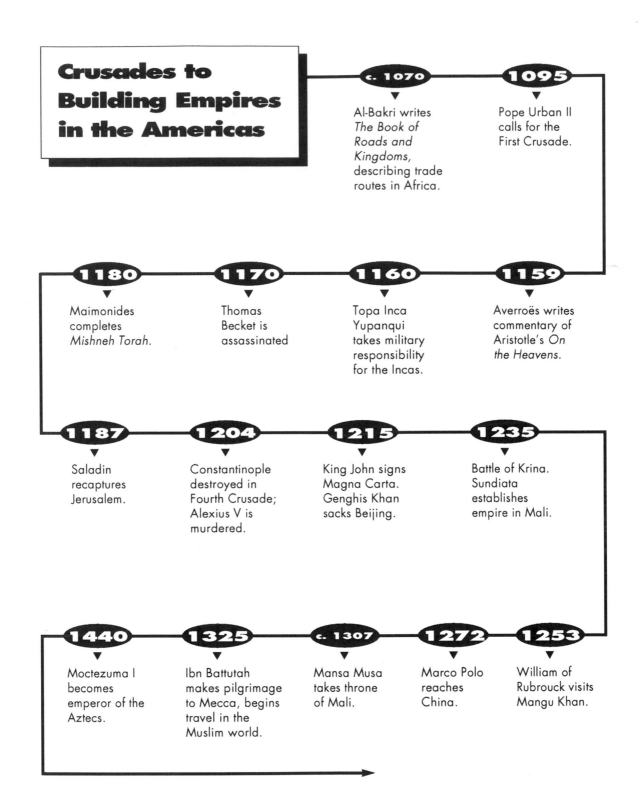

Crusades to Building Empires in the Americas

c. 1070
Al-Bakri writes *The Book of Roads and Kingdoms*, describing trade routes in Africa.

1095
Pope Urban II calls for the First Crusade.

1180
Maimonides completes *Mishneh Torah*.

1170
Thomas Becket is assassinated

1160
Topa Inca Yupanqui takes military responsibility for the Incas.

1159
Averroës writes commentary of Aristotle's *On the Heavens*.

1187
Saladin recaptures Jerusalem.

1204
Constantinople destroyed in Fourth Crusade; Alexius V is murdered.

1215
King John signs Magna Carta. Genghis Khan sacks Beijing.

1235
Battle of Krina. Sundiata establishes empire in Mali.

1440
Moctezuma I becomes emperor of the Aztecs.

1325
Ibn Battutah makes pilgrimage to Mecca, begins travel in the Muslim world.

c. 1307
Mansa Musa takes throne of Mali.

1272
Marco Polo reaches China.

1253
William of Rubrouck visits Mangu Khan.

PROFILES IN WORLD HISTORY

Significant Events and the People

Who Shaped Them

Crusades to Building Empires in the Americas

JOYCE MOSS

and

GEORGE WILSON

AN IMPRINT OF GALE RESEARCH
AN INTERNATIONAL THOMSON PUBLISHING COMPANY

PROFILES IN WORLD HISTORY

Significant Events and the People Who Shaped Them

VOLUME 3: Crusades to Building Empires in the Americas

Joyce Moss and George Wilson

Staff

Carol DeKane Nagel, *U•X•L Developmental Editor*
Julie L. Carnagie, *U•X•L Assistant Editor*
Thomas L. Romig, *U•X•L Publisher*

Shanna P. Heilveil, *Production Assistant*
Evi Seoud, *Assistant Production Manager*
Mary Beth Trimper, *Production Director*

Barbara A. Wallace, *Permissions Associate (Pictures)*

Mary Krzewinski, *Cover and Page Designer*
Cynthia Baldwin, *Art Director*

The Graphix Group, *Typesetting*

∞™ This book is printed on acid-free paper that meets the minimum requirements of American National Standard for Information Sciences—Permanence Paper for Printed Library Materials, ANSI Z39.48-1984.

ISBN 0-7876-0464-X (Set)
ISBN 0-7876-0465-8 (v. 1)   ISBN 0-7876-0469-0 (v. 5)
ISBN 0-7876-0466-6 (v. 2)   ISBN 0-7876-0470-4 (v. 6)
ISBN 0-7876-0467-4 (v. 3)   ISBN 0-7876-0471-2 (v. 7)
ISBN 0-7876-0468-2 (v. 4)   ISBN 0-7876-0472-0 (v. 8)

Printed in the United States of America

I(T)P™ U·X·L is an imprint of Gale Research,
        an International Thomson Publishing Company.
        ITP logo is a trademark under license.

Contents

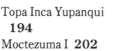

v

Reader's Guide

Profiles in World History: Significant Events and the People Who Shaped Them presents the life stories of more than 175 individuals who have played key roles in world history. The biographies are clustered around 50 broad events, ranging from the Rise of Eastern Religions and Philosophies to the Expansion of World Powers, from Industrial Revolution to Winning African Independence. Each biography—complete in itself—contributes a singular outlook regarding an event; when taken as cluster, the biographies provide a variety of views and experiences, thereby offering a broad perspective on events that shaped the world.

Those whose stories are told in *Profiles in World History* meet one or more of the following criteria. The individuals:

- Represent viewpoints or groups involved in a major world event
- Directly affected the outcome of the event
- Exemplify a role played by common citizens in that event

Format

Profiles in World History volumes are arranged by chapter. Each chapter focuses on one particular event and opens with an overview and detailed time line of the event that places it in historical context. Following are biographical profiles of two to five diverse individuals who played active roles in the event.

Each biographical profile is divided into four sections:

- **Personal Background** provides details that predate and anticipate the individual's involvement in the event

- **Participation** describes the role played by the individual in the event and its impact on his or her life

- **Aftermath** discusses effects of the individual's actions and subsequent relevant events in the person's life

- **For More Information** provides sources for further reading on the individual

Additionally, sidebars containing interesting details about the events and individuals profiled are interspersed throughout the text.

Additional Features

Portraits, illustrations, and maps as well as excerpts from primary source materials are included in *Profiles in World History* to help bring history to life. Sources of all quoted material are cited parenthetically within the text, and complete bibliographic information is listed at the end of each biography. A full bibliography of scholarly sources consulted in preparing each volume appears in each book's back matter.

Cross references are made in the entries, directing readers to other entries within the volume that are connected in some way to the person under scrutiny. Additionally, each volume ends with a subject index, while Volume 8 concludes with a cumulative subject index, providing easy access to the people and events mentioned throughout *Profiles in World History.*

Comments and Suggestions

We welcome your comments on this work as well as your suggestions for individuals to be featured in future editions of *Profiles in World History.* Please write: Editors, *Profiles in World History,* U·X·L, 835 Penobscot Bldg., Detroit, Michigan 48226-4094; fax to 313-961-6348; or call toll-free: 1-800-877-4253.

Acknowledgments

The editors would like to thank the many people involved in the preparation of *Profiles in World History*.

For guidance in the choice of events and personalities, we are grateful to Ross Dunn, Professor of History at the University of California at San Diego, and David Smith, Professor of History at California Polytechnic University at Pomona. We're thankful to Professor Smith for his careful review of the entire series and his guidance toward key sources of information about personalities and events.

We deeply appreciate the writers who compiled data and contributed to the biographies: Diane Ahrens, Bill Boll, Quesiyah Ali Chavez, Charity-Jean Conklin, Mario Cutajar, Craig Hinkel, Hillary Manning, Lawrence Orr, Phillip T. Slattery, Colin Wells, and Susan Yun. We'd especially like to thank Jamie Mohn and Cheryl Steets for their careful attention to the manuscript.

Thanks also to the copy editors and proofreaders, Sonia Benson, Barbara C. Bigelow, Betz Des Chenes, Robert Griffin, Rob Nagel, and Paulette Petrimoulx, for their careful attention to style and detail. Special thanks to Margaret M. Johnson, Judith Kass, and John F. Petruccione for researching the illustrations and maps.

And, finally, thanks to Carol Nagel of U·X·L for overseeing the production of the series.

Picture Credits

The photographs and illustrations appearing in *Profiles in World History: Significant Events and the People Who Shaped Them,* Volume 3: *Crusades to Building Empires in the Americas* were received from the following sources:

On the cover: **The Bettmann Archive:** Genghis Khan; **The Granger Collection:** Marco Polo; **UPI/Bettmann:** King John.

Archive Photos: p. 163; **The Bettmann Archive:** pp. 7, 15, 19, 25, 30, 37, 41, 52, 59, 61, 69, 92, 131, 135, 139, 151, 160, 169, 177, 209; **The Granger Collection:** pp. 79, 81, 95, 103, 117, 126, 129, 132, 183; **Illustrations by Moneta Barnett for *A Glorious Age in Africa* by Daniel Chu and Elliott Skinner, Zenith Books, 1965:** pp. 111, 147; **UPI/Bettmann:** p. 89, 203.

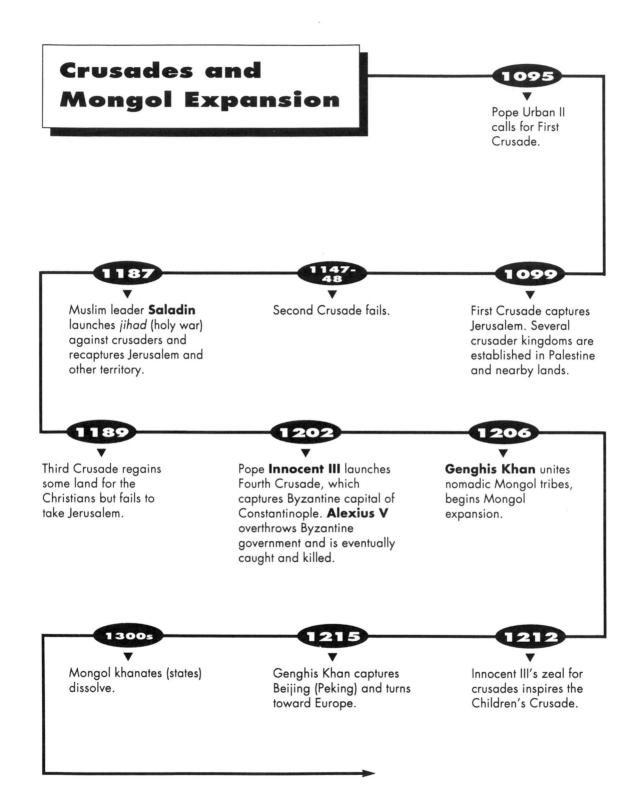

Crusades and Mongol Expansion

1095
Pope Urban II calls for First Crusade.

1099
First Crusade captures Jerusalem. Several crusader kingdoms are established in Palestine and nearby lands.

1147-48
Second Crusade fails.

1187
Muslim leader **Saladin** launches *jihad* (holy war) against crusaders and recaptures Jerusalem and other territory.

1189
Third Crusade regains some land for the Christians but fails to take Jerusalem.

1202
Pope **Innocent III** launches Fourth Crusade, which captures Byzantine capital of Constantinople. **Alexius V** overthrows Byzantine government and is eventually caught and killed.

1206
Genghis Khan unites nomadic Mongol tribes, begins Mongol expansion.

1212
Innocent III's zeal for crusades inspires the Children's Crusade.

1215
Genghis Khan captures Beijing (Peking) and turns toward Europe.

1300s
Mongol khanates (states) dissolve.

CRUSADES AND MONGOL EXPANSION

Two separate campaigns of conquest occurred toward the end of the Middle Ages: the Crusades (in the eleventh to thirteenth centuries) and the expansion of the Mongols (thirteenth to fifteenth centuries). Both were primarily military enterprises that, once over, left little positive evidence of their having occurred. Neither the crusaders nor the Mongols created new cultures or made any significant contributions to existing ones. The crusaders left only some castles behind, while the Mongols left their mark only on the civilizations they damaged or destroyed.

Crusades. The crusaders were Christian Europeans who invaded Palestine to reclaim sites holy to Christians from the Islamic peoples who occupied them. The region had been held by the Muslims for more than three hundred years, and for centuries, Christian pilgrims had journeyed from Europe to the Holy Land of Palestine. There they visited religious sites such as the ancient city of Jerusalem, where many important events in the life of Jesus Christ had taken place. The Islamic rulers of Palestine tolerated the pilgrims for the most part, taxing them but allowing them to travel freely.

The Turks. In the eleventh century, however, territory along the pilgrim's route (Anatolia, now Turkey) was taken over by a

1

new Islamic power, the Turks, who were less tolerant of the Christian travelers. The Turks also threatened the Christian empire of Byzantium, which called on its fellow Christians in Europe for help. (The European [Western] Christians who undertook the Crusades were Catholic; the Christians of the eastern empire of Byzantium were Greek Orthodox [they were descended from the Greeks]. Though both groups were Christian and thus generally allied, differences in religious doctrine and cultural barriers frequently put them at odds.) Pope Urban II launched the Crusades in 1095 by calling on Christians to help the Byzantines and to reclaim the holy places of the East from the Muslims.

Thousands of poor but religiously fervent Christians set out soon afterward, led by Peter the Hermit. Enthusiasm alone, however, could not sustain them on the long and dangerous trip east. Few made it through Turkish-controlled Anatolia. In 1099, however, knights and soldiers succeeded in forcing their way through. Population growth in Europe and the promise of wealth in the rich East drew adventurous young men who were well suited to a military crusade. Many were younger sons of nobles, knights who sought their fortunes in the Crusades because, according to custom, their older brothers had inherited the family wealth.

The knights and soldiers of the First Crusade reached Constantinople, the capital of Byzantium and eastern seat of the Catholic Church, in 1096. The city was already under siege by Norman invaders from Europe and threatened by Turkish advances from the East. Because of this, the emperor of Byzantium, Alexius I, was first forced to join in support of the crusaders in order to oust the Normans and Turks, and then to engage in a war against them to regain control of the city. Though beaten in Constantinople, the crusaders went on to capture a strip of land along the coast of Palestine, which included many important cities. Among them was Jerusalem, the crusaders' main target.

◄

Crusade fever gripped Europe in the twelfth century; this depiction of a peasants' crusade is from a French manuscript titled *Livres des Passages d'Outremer.*

▲ **The ancient city of Jerusalem, the crusaders' main target, after the Crusades; it continues to be held holy by Jews, Christians, and Muslims.**

To defend their newly won territory, the crusaders built huge stone castles in which they could hold off Muslim attacks. As for the Muslims, their own political struggles stopped them from mounting much resistance to the crusaders. While the crusaders stood united under strong leadership, the Muslims struggled for power among themselves in the lands surrounding the new crusader kingdoms.

The situation reversed itself within a century, however. By the 1170s Egypt, Syria, and Mesopotamia—that is, all the lands surrounding the crusaders—were united under a single powerful Muslim leader, **Saladin.**

Saladin launched his own crusade, the *jihad,* or Muslim holy war. He succeeded in recapturing Jerusalem and other territory. Though the Third Crusade, beginning in 1189, won back some of the disputed land, the crusaders did not regain their former position of dominance in Palestine.

In 1202 Pope **Innocent III** launched the Fourth Crusade, which achieved little against the Muslims. Instead, the crusaders were sidetracked by another seige—this one successful—of Constantinople, the rulers of which were supposedly the crusaders' Christian allies. Despite the best efforts of **Alexius V,** a Byzantine politician, the Latin (Catholic) kingdom of Constantinople endured from 1204 to 1261, when the Byzantines recaptured the city.

The Mongols. Beginning in the early thirteenth century, the Mongol leader **Genghis Khan** forged a fearsome fighting force out of the nomadic tribesmen of central Asia. Demonstrating superior fighting skills, these mounted warriors undertook one of the most remarkable campaigns of conquest in history, covering a huge expanse of territory from China to the Black Sea, and from Siberia to Tibet. After directing marches against Muslim cities in the Middle East, Genghis turned toward Europe. East European monarchs, panicked by the advancing Mongols, asked the popes who succeeded Innocent III for protection. This resulted in correspondence between popes and Mongol leaders for several decades, but no direct confrontations ever occurred. By about 1221 the Mongol forces had reached present-day Romania and were threatening Hungary. Prohibitively lengthy supply lines, however, forced them to turn back.

Holy Land
Jerusalem is sacred to the Jews as the site of an ancient temple, the most holy of places. It also has religious importance for Christians and Muslims. For Christians, it is the site of many events in the life of Jesus Christ. For Muslims, it is where Muhammad is believed to have risen to heaven. Jerusalem is home to historic synagogues, churches, and mosques.

Though several Mongol empires were carved out of these conquests after Genghis Khan's death, Mongol power had largely disappeared by the beginning of the fifteenth century. Its significance lies mostly in its effect on the conquered peoples. For example, Mongol conquest of southern Russia changed that country's history dramatically by cutting it off from the rest of Europe.

Saladin

c. 1138-1193

Personal Background

The man known in the West as Saladin was born Yusuf ibn Ayyub ("Joseph the Son of Ayyub") in the town of Tikrit in present-day Iraq. "Saladin" is the English version of *Salah al-din,* Arabic for "honoring the faith," and is one of several names Yusef ibn Ayyub took for himself in the custom of Muslim rulers. He was not born into a ruling family, however. His father, Ayyub, was a Kurdish soldier serving the caliph, one of Islam's supreme rulers, who governed from the capital of Baghdad (now capital of Iraq). Ayyub was in charge of the small town of Tikrit and of the soldiers stationed there.

To Syria. On the night Saladin was born Ayyub and his family left Tikrit. They eventually settled in Baalbek, Syria, near the Mediterranean coast, far to the west of Saladin's birthplace. There Ayyub acted as local governor for Syria's ruler, Zengi, and there Saladin was raised and educated. After Zengi's death in 1146, Nur al-din, Zengi's son and successor, kept Ayyub on as governor of Baalbek. He also put Ayyub in command of the defense force in nearby Damascus, the Syrian capital and the Islamic world's second-most important city.

Not far to the west of Damascus lay a coastal strip of land that stretched from Antioch in the north, through Tripoli and Beirut, and to Jerusalem in the south. This narrow strip was cap-

▲ Saladin

Event: Resisting the Crusades.

Role: From his power base in Egypt, the Muslim warrior Saladin won control of much of the Islamic Middle East. He was then able to begin the Muslim push to win back territory, including the cities of Jerusalem and Acre, that had been taken by Christians during the First Crusade of 1099. Though the Third Crusade under Richard I recaptured Acre, the crusaders would never regain their dominance in the Holy Land.

tured by Christians during the First Crusade in 1099. Though it was surrounded by Muslim territory, it remained in the hands of the crusaders because unlike the Muslims, they were united under strong leadership.

Years of training. Damascus was the target of the Second Crusade, launched in 1147, two years after Ayyub and his family arrived there. Led by the rulers of Germany and France, the crusade failed, and Nur al-din's power grew stronger. In 1152 the fourteen-year-old Saladin was sent to Aleppo, another Syrian city, to help his uncle Shirkuh, who, like Ayyub, was one of Nur al-din's commanders. In Aleppo, Saladin continued his education, adding military training to his study of Islamic religion and culture. When Shirkuh was made governor of Damascus a few years later, Saladin was assigned to be his uncle's deputy. For the next several years, Saladin was in charge of keeping order in Damascus and overseeing the punishment of criminals, among other duties.

Participation: Resisting the Crusades

Egyptian expedition. In 1164 civil war broke out in Egypt between two of the country's Islamic rulers. One of the two rivals, Shawer, fled to Damascus, appealing to Nur al-din for help. In return Shawer promised future payment to Nur al-din of a third of his yearly tax revenues. Accepting the deal, Nur al-din sent his commander Shirkuh with an army to Egypt. Saladin, now in his late twenties, went along as the officer responsible for keeping the expedition supplied with food, clothing, and equipment.

As soon as he was returned to power by Shirkuh's army, Shawer reneged on his promise to Nur al-din. He then offered to pay the crusaders, who had taken advantage of the civil war to attack Egypt, if they would fight against Shirkuh, who had become his enemy as a result of being cheated. Thus Shirkuh and Saladin were forced to defend against the invading crusader army, as well as the unreliable and now hostile Shawer.

Battle command. Before a confrontation could develop, however, both armies found themselves marching, almost within

▲ **Saladin in battle; in the short space of several months, Saladin had gone from minor military commander to national ruler.**

sight of each other, north to Palestine. There, south of Syria, Nur al-din had launched an attack on crusader territory.

Shirkuh advised Nur al-din to focus again on gaining control of Egypt. Nur al-din agreed, and in 1167 Shirkuh and Saladin led another force south, where they battled the combined Egyptian and crusader armies. Saladin, commanding the center of the battle line, followed his uncle's instructions and pretended to retreat. It was a trick Muslims had used before against the heavily armored crusaders, and, as usual, it worked. When the crusaders followed Saladin behind a hill, Shirkuh ambushed them with the Turkish cavalry he had recruited to support him.

Siege and chivalry. After the resulting victory, Shirkuh marched north and took over the key Egyptian city of Alexandria. When the remaining crusaders besieged the city, Shirkuh escaped with most of his army, leaving Saladin in command with a thousand men. But as the food ran out, both civilians and soldiers were threatened with starvation. Saladin sent a message to Shirkuh, outside the city, suggesting a meeting with the crusaders to discuss a peace agreement. The crusaders agreed, and Saladin himself visited the crusader camp during the discussions.

There he was received according to the crusader knights' traditions of chivalry, or knightly manners. One story has it that Saladin himself was knighted by a crusader noble—it was all very friendly and respectful, as was the custom when a knight was presented to an enemy commander. Later in his career, Saladin's own version of chivalry would win him a place in the history of Western culture, a place unique among Muslim leaders.

Ruler of Egypt. Within two years, Saladin and Shirkuh were again forced to confront the crusaders, who had once more set their sights on Egypt. Egypt's Fatimid Caliph (the nation's supreme religious leader, head of the Shiite sect) and Shawer, now its vizier (prime minister), appealed to Nur al-din for help. In early 1169 Shirkuh and Saladin set out with a large army. Soon after their arrival, the treacherous Shawer was arrested and executed for plotting Shirkuh's murder. The caliph chose Shirkuh as vizier in Shawer's place, but two months later, Shirkuh himself died suddenly. The office of vizier was open again, and this time it was awarded to Saladin, who was nominated by the dying Shirkuh. In the short space of several months, Saladin had gone from minor commander to national ruler. He was about thirty years old.

Taking control. During the following two years, Saladin was occupied with maintaining his power in an always complicated and often dangerous political environment. As soon as he had crushed a mutiny in the Egyptian army, he faced a massive invasion by combined forces of the crusaders and their Christian ally in the eastern Mediterranean, the Byzantine Empire. The Byzantines' powerful navy supported the crusader army. Only bad weather, which had bogged down the crusaders and delayed allied ships, saved Saladin from a major defeat.

Then, in 1171, the Fatimid Caliph died. His death gave Saladin a chance to promote unity within the Islamic world and to strengthen his own position. The Fatimid (Shiite) caliphs had competed with the Sunni caliphs of Baghdad for the right to claim supreme authority in the name of Muhammad, the founder of Islam. Nur al-din had been loyal to Baghdad, as had Ayyub (still a trusted adviser) and Shirkuh. But in accepting power from the Fatimid Caliph of Egypt, Shirkuh and then Saladin had risked seeming disloyal to Nur al-din and to the caliph in Baghdad. Now, with the Fatimid Caliph dead, Saladin seized the luxurious Fatimid palaces and put the caliph's family under arrest, ending the almost three-hundred-year-long Fatimid dynasty (family rule).

Death of Nur al-din. In 1174 first Ayyub and then Nur al-din died, Nur al-din leaving an eleven-year-old son as his only heir. Syria was thrown into turmoil as various local leaders competed for power. As war threatened to break out between Aleppo and Damascus, the ruler of Damascus wrote Saladin that an attempt by him to take over Damascus would be popular among its citizens. It was another opportunity for Saladin to promote unity within the Islamic world—and to strengthen his own position. With a force of only seven hundred horsemen, Saladin rode north through Palestine to Damascus, where the people gave him a warm welcome. (It was all the warmer because Saladin handed out large gifts from Nur al-din's treasury.) During the rest of the year, he conquered the other major cities of Syria, all except Aleppo, which held out against him.

> ### Shiite and Sunni
>
> Like the Christian crusaders, who were split into Catholics (Westerners) and their Greek Orthodox (Byzantine; descended from the Greeks) allies, the Islamic world was also divided by religious beliefs. The Fatimids, whom Saladin overthrew, were Shiites, which meant that they supported their own caliph instead of the Sunni Caliph in Baghdad. The dispute goes back to Islam's early days, and Shiites (though a minority today, dominant only in Iran) continue to differ from the majority Sunnis.

Expansion. During the next decade or so, Saladin first strengthened his rule in Egypt and Syria, then began expanding his territory eastward. He conquered Aleppo in 1183, and two years later won over the important city of Mosul in Mesopotamia (now Iraq). During this period, he also won several battles with the crusaders. By the late 1180s he was the most powerful ruler in the Islamic world, in firm control of Egypt, Syria, and Mesopotamia.

Jihad. As Islam's strongest ruler, Saladin was now ready to lead the fight to win back territory lost in the First Crusade almost a century before. The largest and most powerful crusader kingdom was the Kingdom of Jerusalem, earlier united under a strong king. Now, however, civil war was threatening to break out among the crusader leaders, while the surrounding Muslims were finally united under Saladin's leadership. In 1187 Saladin sent out a call for *jihad,* or holy war, against the Christians. The idea of a holy war, a war for religious reasons, had been introduced by Muhammad himself and therefore had a traditional place in Islamic society. Warriors killed in such a war are believed to be rewarded with everlasting life in paradise. Now Saladin called on the Muslim faithful and vowed to capture the holy city of Jerusalem.

Ayyubid Dynasty

According to Muslim custom, Saladin had several wives—among them a former wife of Nur al-din's—and fathered perhaps seventeen children. Both his older sons and his brothers helped him in governing the large areas under his control. This "Ayyubid Dynasty," so-called because the common ancestor was Saladin's father, Ayyub, continued to oppose the crusaders after Saladin's death. Ayyubid power, though, gradually broke up, ending around 1250.

Battle of Hattin. Both sides began gathering their forces as the summer of 1187 approached. Finally, in the heat of the summer, Saladin led his army into crusader territory and took a position south of the small town of Hattin, near Nazareth. There he waited. The crusader army, camped twenty-five miles away, hesitated. Some wanted to attack, but others warned that there was no water between the two armies—with their heavy armor, the knights would be exhausted by a long march through the hot, dusty desert. Nonetheless, the attack was mounted. Saladin sent out archers, who shot arrows into the crusaders' ranks as they marched, slowing them down. By the time they arrived at the front, the crusaders were tired, thirsty, and discouraged. In the battle that followed, the entire crusader army, despite their stubborn fighting, was killed or taken prisoner, to be traded for payment or in exchange for Muslim prisoners. Saladin's victory had shattered the crusaders' power.

Capture of Jerusalem. With the crusader army smashed, the coastal cities they had supported could no longer hold off the Muslim advance, and most of Palestine was soon back in Muslim hands. The cities surrendered all the more easily because Saladin offered them unusually generous terms and then kept his promises. Word got around that the Muslim commander would spare people's lives and even let them leave with their belongings, unlike the crusaders when they captured the same cities in 1099. On October 2, 1187, Jerusalem surrendered on such terms. Saladin's soldiers complained that they weren't allowed to plunder the cities, as was customary. Saladin's reputation for honesty and fairness grew not only among Muslims but among the crusaders as well.

Third Crusade. In response to Saladin's conquests, Europe launched the Third Crusade in 1189, under Germany's Frederick I and England's Richard I, also known as Richard the Lion-Hearted. Frederick, however, drowned on the long journey from Europe to Palestine. His powerful army broke up, and few of his soldiers finished the trip. Despite Richard's strong leadership, the Third Crusade was able to do little more than recapture (in 1191) the city of Acre (in present-day Israel), along with a strip of coast and one or two other cities.

Aftermath

Damascus. Years of hard marching and fighting had taken its toll, and though only in his mid-fifties, Saladin was no longer a healthy man. His carefully trimmed black beard was streaked with grey, his average-size but wiry body had lost its powers of endurance, and he had long suffered from stomach problems. With the end of the Third Crusade, Saladin returned to Damascus, where he died in 1193, at the age of fifty-five.

For More Information

Ehrenkreutz, Andrew. *Saladin.* Albany: State University of New York Press, 1972.

Gibb, Hamilton. *The Life of Saladin.* Oxford, England: Oxford University Press, 1973.

Newby, P. H. *Saladin in His Time.* London: Faber & Faber, 1983.

Genghis Khan

c. 1162-1227

Personal Background

Mongol life. That part of Asia lying just south and east of
Lake Baikal is a flat grassland called the Mongolian Plateau. It is a
land of scorching heat and bitter cold. Here, long ago, the nomads
(now called Mongols) gathered in tribes. They herded cattle,
sheep, and horses and depended on their animals for food, shelter,
and clothing. The sheep gave them wool from which they made a
thick felt. Stretched over rounded poles, the felt made dome-
shaped tents that protected them from the cold. Animal furs provided two sets of clothing, one worn fur side in and the other fur
side out to protect against the wind and weather. Milk came from
their mares. Other food came from the hunt. The Mongols spent
many hours hunting and perhaps as many fighting, and it was
sometimes easier to raid a neighbor for food than to hunt or fish.
Most of the Mongols were warriors and preferred to fight.

There were many tribes of Mongols. One group called itself
Neyrum, or Great Mongols, and followed the warrior Yekusai.
Aided by his strong and wise wife, Houlun, Yekusai ruled over
forty thousand tents, a small number compared to his neighbors
and enemies. His tent, like those of lesser leaders, was decorated
outside as befitted a khan, or leader. It was mounted on a cart so
that cattle could be quickly harnessed and the home moved, for
the tribe moved often in search of food.

▲ **Genghis Khan**

Event: The invasion of the Middle East.

Role: Having taken control of most of China and the land north of Mongolia, Genghis Khan tried to form trading agreements with the Muslim leader of southern Turkistan. When that failed, the khan launched an attack that took the Mongol warriors as far west as Russia.

Everyone had to work to survive. While Yekusai and the strongest men hunted and fought, the girls and women tended the home, guarded the family wealth stored inside, and drove the cattle pulling the wide, flat wagons. The boys tended the herds of horses, sheep, or cattle. All the children of the Neyrum added to the family food supply by hunting rodents and other small animals.

The boys honed their skills early on so they could join the tribe's warriors. They learned to ride by climbing on the backs of sheep and holding on to the long fur. While still quite young, they learned to ride horses and to travel with little or no food for as long as a raid lasted.

Birth of Temujin. In 1162, Yekusai led a raid on the Tatar tribe of his enemy Temujin. It was a successful raid; Temujin was taken prisoner and his tribe destroyed. Some were killed, while others chose to join Yekusai's warriors and become Neyrums. The victorious khan returned home to find that Houlun had delivered him a son.

With the passing of time wondrous stories have grown about this child. One folktale tells how Yekusai took the child's hand only to find that it held firmly to a clot of blood. The clot seemed to be a red stone and was taken as a symbol that the tribe would continue to be victorious over the Tatars. Yekusai celebrated his victory and the omen by naming his first son Temujin after his brave enemy.

The young Genghis. Temujin grew to be a slender boy with light brown skin, reddish brown hair, and blue-gray eyes. Though thin, the boy was strong like his father and crafty like his mother. His skill and strength served him well in the games of the tribe—games such as horseback races that took participants miles away from the settlement and back, or wrestling, which often continued until an opponent was knocked unconscious or had broken bones. Temujin excelled at these games, as he knew he should. After all, his ancestor was the Kabal Khan, who had been brave enough to have once pulled the beard of the powerful ruler of Cathay (China). Temujin seemed to have inherited his ancestor's hot temper as well as his courage. One story tells of Temujin beating a half-brother to death because he had stolen one of Temujin's fish.

Mostly, though, the boy was a quiet young man, given more

to listening than talking. Sitting around the campfires at night, Neyrum boys listened to tales of great raids of the past. One of these raids had brought Temujin's mother to the Neyrum—she had been kidnapped from a neighboring tribe.

Betrothal. By the time he was thirteen years old, Temujin was riding with his father on raids and visits to neighbors. On one such visit, he could not help but notice the daughter of the host. Although she was only nine years old, Bourtai was already beautiful. In the tradition of the Neyrum, Temujin asked his father if he could marry her. The girl was too young for marriage, but the families made marriage arrangements. Temujin would stay with Bourtai's family until she was of age.

The new khan. Yekusai headed home. A few days later a messenger brought Temujin news that his father had been poisoned by some enemies. Riding as quickly as possible, he nonetheless failed to reach his father before he died. Temujin was now in line to become khan of the Neyrum. That title had to be earned, however, as he soon learned.

When they heard of Yekusai's death, some of the chiefs who had been loyal to him decided that the inexperienced Temujin would not be strong enough to protect them. Houlon had tried to persuade them to remain with the tribe; she had taken up the Neyrum standard of nine yak tails and spoken heatedly to keep the loyalty of the chiefs. Some were persuaded, but most joined the powerful Taidjuts. The khan of the Taidjuts, Targoutai, claimed that he reigned over all the Northern Gobi region. Temujin was a threat to this claim; he needed to be found and destroyed.

Building as a leader. The Taidjuts were much stronger than the Neyrum, so Temujin and his small band were in great danger. He and his brothers avoided the Taidjut search for days, but Temujin was finally caught trying to obtain food. Wary of the boy's strength, Targoutai ordered the young khan bound to a heavy wooden yoke and kept under guard in the center of the Taidjut village.

Temujin, however, planned to escape, return to his people, and build a new army. When all was quiet near the tent in which he was held, the powerful Neyrum raised up and crashed the heavy yoke on the head of his guard. Then he ran, still bound to the yoke, to a nearby river and hid in water up to his nose. Taidjut warriors searched for him. One even seemed to notice him in the water but said nothing. After a short search, the Taidjuts rested; they didn't think Temujin could go far bound to the heavy yoke.

Still heavily bound, Temujin took the only chance he thought possible to escape. In the dark of night, he returned to the enemy village and found the tent of the man who had seen him in the water. He hoped that this man would help him. As it was, the Taidjut warrior had no choice—if Temujin was found in his tent, it would mean death. So he helped Temujin out of the yoke and broke it up for firewood. Then he borrowed a horse to aid in Temujin's escape.

Khan of the Neyrum. Back home, Temujin found that neighbors had spread the word of his bold escape. More Neyrum began to accept him as their leader. Slowly he began to build and train an army. After a few years, he had acquired enough power to take Bourtai, now thirteen, as his wife. In their life together, she would bear him four sons. He would have other wives, some say as many as five hundred, but Temujin recognized no heirs other than the sons of Bourtai.

Temujin might have asked for help from his godfather, Toghrul, leader of the Karaits, but he waited. He wanted to go to him only when the Neyrum and Karaits were equal in strength. Before he could become that strong, however, the northern Merkits, the tribe from which his mother had been stolen, launched a surprise attack on his settlement. Temujin was able to find a horse and escape, but Bourtai was captured and given to the man from whom Temujin's mother had been stolen. Now Temujin asked for help from Toghrul, and the two raided the Merkit camp and rescued Bourtai.

For the next several years, Temujin fought with one neighbor and then another, protecting his land and capturing enemies to build up his own armies. Several times he was wounded by the eastern Taidjuts and Tatars. Once he was left for dead in the snow. Every adventure seemed to make him more important in the eyes of the Mongol tribes.

▲ Armed Mongols assembling for conquest; most of the Mongols were warriors and preferred fighting over hunting.

Participation: Building a Mongol Nation

War with the Taidjuts. Temujin's most dangerous enemy remained the Taidjuts led by Targoutai. When he learned they were advancing with a force of thirty thousand warriors, Temujin showed his military genius. He had only thirteen thousand warriors, so he chose a narrow valley for the battle. The Taidjuts advanced in squadrons of five hundred men, with lines five deep. Against this, Temujin threw his forces in double squadrons and ten men deep. That made his front lines stronger than the enemy's. He had only thirteen fighting units and his foe had sixty, but the enemy's units could not all fight at the same time on the narrow battlefield.

The great armies fought all day with bows and arrows, sabres, lariats, and lances tipped with hooks. Temujin won a great victory. Perhaps six thousand Taidjuts were killed or injured. Seventy enemy chiefs were captured and led before the khan with their swords and quivers dangling from their necks in submission. Though legend has it that they were boiled alive on the spot, it is unlikely that this happened. Temujin was cruel in war as was common in his day, but he also needed good men.

King of kings. Now Temujin dreamed of greater power. In 1206 he called a meeting of neighboring khans at the Onon River. He told them that larger and fiercer tribes would continue to threaten unless all the smaller tribes banded together. Always a good speaker, he convinced the other khans to place him above themselves as the chief ruler of the area. Another legend tells how an important medicine man announced to the group that Temujin would thereafter be known as Genghis Kha Khan, the Emperor of All Men. That is how the council left the matter.

The group over which Genghis Khan now presided represented many societies and many cultures that had one thing in common: they were accustomed to warring against each other. Nevertheless, Genghis was determined to unite them into one people. He began by insisting on a common language. One of the conquered groups, the Uigurs, had a written language. Genghis ordered that their alphabet be used to create a Neyrum written language. Although there is no evidence that he used the written language himself, he hired Uigur teachers for his sons.

The lawgiver. Genghis Khan then set about organizing the masses. Every ten men formed a fighting unit sworn to help each other in times of need. These tens were assembled into groups of one hundred, who, in turn, were organized into groups of one thousand, and so on. The best men from fourteen to sixty years old were in the army. All military men and citizens were governed by strict laws that were upheld by Genghis Khan's private army. Death was the penalty for a warrior who failed to help a fallen brother in battle or failed to join in the fighting. Theft and adultery were also punished by death. It was said that a stranger could walk from one end of Genghis Khan's territory to the other without fear of being robbed or attacked.

To protect the empire and to encourage loyalty, all soldiers were required to store their weapons in a government warehouse between battles or hunts. In return, each soldier was allowed to keep whatever loot he took from an enemy, save for a tax for the khan, of course. It was only forbidden to take another Mongol into slavery.

While most of the peoples of Asia believed in more than one god, many Mongols believed in a single all-powerful Sky or Heaven god. Genghis's laws began, "It is ordered to believe that there is only one God, creator of heaven and earth, who alone gives life and death, riches and poverty as pleases Him—and who has over everything an absolute power" (Lamb 1927, p. 201).

Quarrel with Cathay. There remained one major foe in the East. South and east, beyond the Great Wall, lay the empire of Cathay. (The Wall had been built to protect Cathay from "barbarian" enemies.) Rich in trade, culture, and buildings, and strong in soldiers and weapons, this empire had long demanded tribute from the weaker tribes of the Mongols, and the emperor of Cathay now expected payments from Genghis Khan. By this time, Genghis Khan had a fighting force of more than a hundred thousand soldiers. In 1211 they broke through the Wall and spread down its length toward the Cathay capital (now Beijing). For six years, the two empires battled, until three of the khan's armies, led by his sons and brothers, conquered the land west to the sea and south to present-day Henan. Beijng was subdued in 1215.

How Complete Were Genghis Khan's Laws?

Most Mongols were very afraid of lightning and would jump in the nearest river or lake to avoid it. Genghis Khan remedied this by forbidding anyone to touch bodies of water in a storm. The Yassa, Genghis Khan's set of laws, described what people were free to do. For example, Genghis Khan hated drinking, but the laws permitted a Mongol man to get drunk three times a month. The Yassa also prescribed ways to do business (bartering was frowned on) and ways of settling quarrels. Above all, no one was allowed to think about becoming another Genghis Khan.

Europe and the Middle East. Genghis Khan now had enough land for himself and his sons. He decided to turn his attention to trade and wrote to the Muslim leaders in the Middle East that he had no more plans to take land. He sent ambassadors to establish trade agreements, but these ambassadors were treated rudely and sometimes cruelly.

Genghis Khan's rage took over. With an army of a quarter of a million warriors, he directed marches against the Muslim cities.

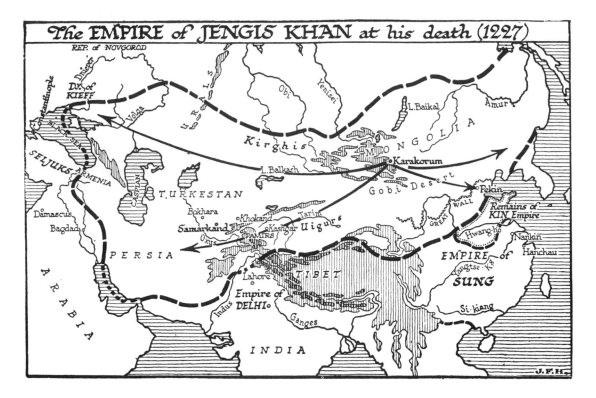

The EMPIRE of JENGIS KHAN at his death (1227)

▲ The empire of Genghis Khan at the time of his death, 1227.

Although his fighting units were often not as large as the enemy's, Genghis Khan's soldiers were highly organized and very effective. Hundreds of miles from home, Mongol soldiers could not manage prisoners, but to leave behind an enemy that might rebuild an army was equally untenable. They were required to live off the land they captured. The soldiers therefore took what they wanted and destroyed the rest, killing those they'd defeated. Whole cities, Samarkand and Kiev among them, were completely destroyed. Some reports estimate that the fight against the city of Merv killed 1,500,000 of its citizens. Genghis Khan had come to believe that he was directed by Heaven to fight and destroy his enemies.

After several more years of fighting, Genghis Khan's empire spread from Korea to European Russia and from the far north nearly to the border of India. Europe seemed on the brink of a Mongol invasion. Through it all, Genghis Khan claimed that he had no control over what happened. Heaven or Sky determined the actions of the Mongols.

Aftermath

The end of the Mongol threat. In 1221, the aging Genghis Khan took personal command of his armies as they marched across Persia and into Russia, plundering the land of the Volga and Dnieper rivers. He had caused a great deal of anxiety in Europe. Some of the kings there had thought that the Mongol hordes would continue to sweep westward and take all of Europe. Some believed that a Mongol invasion was an act of God directed against them for their own evil deeds. But as suddenly as he had come, Genghis Khan changed his course and started home to Karakorum in central Mongolia.

Death. For a short time, the warriors rested. But then Genghis Khan turned his armies loose on the kingdom of Tanjout (now southwest China). The king of Tanjout finally agreed to submit to the great khan, but before he could do that, Genghis died. The date of his death has been given as August 24, 1227.

> ### Fear of the Mongols
>
> Mongol warriors seemed fearless, and because they had learned to use their bows and arrows while riding horses, they seemed unbeatable. Many folk stories arose about their power and the fear it inspired. A story was told of a group of seventeen approached by a lone Mongol. That warrior told the seventeen to take turns tying each other up to be more easily killed. Out of fear, they did.

The empire continues. Genghis Khan's empire survived after his death. In accordance with the terms of his will, his eldest son became the Lord of Lords and presided over Bourtai and Genghis's other three sons, each of whom had his own section of the empire. Parts of these empires eventually fell to Genghis Khan's grandsons. One of them, Kublai Khan, is credited with uniting all of present-day China.

For More Information

Blunt, Wilfred. *The Golden Road to Samarkand.* New York: Viking Press, 1973.

Grousset, Rene. *Conqueror of the World.* New York: Orion Press, 1966.

Lamb, Harold. *Genghis Khan.* Garden City, New York: Garden City Press, 1927.

Innocent III

c. 1161-1216

Personal Background

The family. Lothair del Conti de Segni was born about 1161 at Anagni, roughly thirty-five miles southeast of Rome. His parents were wealthy landowners from noble families. Lothair's father was a descendent of the wealthy Conti family and bore the title Trasmund of Segni; his mother, Clarisia, was the daughter of the noble family of Scotti.

Early life. The young Lothair, therefore, had a privileged upbringing. He attended the best schools in Rome before going off to the universities in Paris and Bologna. His uncle, Clement III, had been pope of the Roman Catholic Church, and Lothair studied to follow him in church service. He learned church and public law and at the same time became well educated in the principles and rituals of the church. Throughout his life, Lothair would hold all the sacraments of the church, including marriage, unbreakable.

Work for the church. Lothair's great knowledge of both church and lay law was recognized soon after his university days. He first served as canon (a lay leader) of St. Peter's Church. Later he took a job with the Roman Curia (governing council), then became subdeacon (a sort of clerk) of the Catholic Church and deacon to the cardinals. He also wrote three books. The best known of these is titled *On Contempt for the World,* about the evils of breaking the rules of the church.

▲ Innocent III

Event: Unifying Europe.

Role: Pope Innocent III claimed to be directed by God to rule the world. By the time of his death, he had power over Europe as far as the ancient realm of Hungary and had extended his authority as pope to the Church in Constantinople.

Pope Innocent III. In 1198 Pope Celestine III died, and the cardinals gathered to elect a new pope. A few thought the thirty-seven-year-old Lothair was too young. Besides, he had not yet qualified to become a priest. Nevertheless, his leadership and legal skills were needed, and he was elected pope on January 8, 1198, taking the name Innocent III. In February he was made a priest and the next day was promoted to bishop.

The position of pope was not as important as it had been in earlier times. The Church itself had broken into a great number of smaller sects. The pope's influence in Europe had been taken over by kings and princes who, themselves, had only a little power over the many noblemen.

Earlier popes had come to control a band of states across Italy that surrounded Rome. By Innocent III's time, however, these "Papal States" had fallen under the rule of local nobles. Even in Rome, Church leaders had lost control of the city. The taxes from Rome and the Papal States that the church had once claimed were paid to local politicians.

Participation: Unifying the Catholic World

Politics. Innocent III set out to regain the power of the ancient Church. First, he would reclaim Rome. By clever use of the law and by pitting one politician against another, he succeeded in replacing the prefect in charge of Rome with a manager appointed by him. The tax monies from Rome began to flow into the Church treasury once more. Innocent used these taxes to buy land south and east of Rome for better protection of the city. He reclaimed the Papal States by using two powerful tools of the Church—interdiction and excommunication. A person under interdict could not take part in the sacraments of the Church. That person could not be married officially in the church, nor could he or she be buried by the Church. Excommunication simply meant that the person was banished from the Church altogether. Using these actions against those who didn't support the Church, supporting friendly rulers, and buying land, Innocent gradually increased the wealth of the Church and regained control of the states around Rome. By 1202 the pope was strong enough to once more claim the sole right to crown the emperor of the Holy Roman Empire.

Otto IV. Soon the chance came for Innocent to regain the Church's former power in Europe. Otto IV was the son of Henry, Duke of Saxony, and nephew of King Richard I (Richard the Lion-Hearted) of England. He was chosen by the Germanic peoples in northern Italy to be their king. Also contending for this crown was Philip of Swabia. Innocent sided with Otto, who was crowned in 1209.

Innocent soon regretted taking Otto's side. The new king quickly began to assume powers the pope had reserved for himself. Otto's greed soon showed in another place. He wanted to claim the land of the two Sicilys (the island of Sicily and mainland Italy from Naples south). That was papal territory; the pope and the king began to quarrel.

Frederick II. Henry VI had been king of Sicily, and his widow, Constance, was a very devout Catholic. She willed not only Sicily but her own baby son to the pope. The son, Frederick II, was made a ward of the pope and crowned King of Sicily when he was four years old, in 1198. He too would prove to be a disappointment to the Church, though Innocent defended him his entire life.

Meanwhile, Innocent continued to build power for the Church and the pope throughout Europe. To do this, he further relied on the rules of the church and threatened interdicts and excommunications for those kings who failed to live up to the rules. Nor was Innocent shy about using the military might of the Church and its subject kings. He also used the Crusades to eliminate opposition to his rule.

Interdiction and Excommunication as Weapons

- Declared interdict to stop Philip Augustus, who planned to abandon his wife to marry a younger woman.
- Declared interdict on Alfonso IX, king of Leon, for misusing Church property.
- Excommunicated German King Otto IV for opposing the church's plans in Sicily and for claiming authority over the pope's subjects.
- Placed interdicts on King John of England for stealing Church property. (This interdict encouraged John to accept the Magna Carta in 1215.) Innocent III then opposed the Magna Carta as diminishing his authority.
- Approved interdicts and punishments for speakers against the Church. This later resulted in the Spanish Inquisition.

A new crusade. Early in his rule, Innocent had called for a Fourth Crusade to once more free Jerusalem from the Muslims. Knights and princes from all of Europe answered the call and formed great armies. They were to sail from Venice but arrived there to find they could not afford the price of the ships. There was a great delay while the leaders of the Crusade bargained with the city, agreeing to pay for the needed ships by capturing another trade city, opposite Venice across the Adriatic Sea, and placing it under the control of Dandolo, the ruler of Venice. That city was Constantinople.

As the capital of the Byzantine Empire, which separated Europe from Asia and the Middle East, Constantinople was at the crossroads of Eastern and Western cultures. Because of its location at this nexus, the city had become an important trade center and perhaps the richest metropolis in the world.

When the ships finally sailed from Venice in 1202, they headed not for Jerusalem or Egypt, home of other holy sites, but for Susa and then Constantinople. Dandolo had arranged for the ships to change course and personally led the crusaders to the capital of Byzantium. The crusaders installed rulers sympathetic to them to preside over Byzantium. (The European [Western] Christians who undertook the Crusades were Catholic and guided by the authority of the pope; the Christians of the eastern empire of Byzantium were Greek Orthodox [they were descended from the Greeks]. Though both groups were Christian and thus generally allied, differences in religious doctrine and cultural barriers frequently put them at odds.) A year later, the crusaders sacked Constantinople, Rome effectively occupying it until 1261, when the Byzantines gained control.

Innocent, now effectively in control of both Catholic Europe and the Byzantine Empire, was on his way to ruling the world. He had told the cardinals, "The Lord entrusted to Peter the government not only of the whole Church, but of the whole world" (Gontard, p. 258). But standing in Innocent's way were the unruly kings of Europe, the Muslims of the Middle East, and farther east, another man who thought Heaven had sent him to rule the world, **Genghis Khan** (see entry) of the Mongols.

▲ A crusader praying for protection during battle; as Pope Innocent's power grew, he became a dictator.

▲ Crusader boys on their way to free the Holy Land; the Children's Crusade, as it came to be known, shocked Innocent but did not turn him against crusading.

Local crusades. As his power grew, Innocent became a dictator. When people spoke against his ideas, the pope raged. No one was allowed to speak in church or about the Church unless approved by one of the pope's bishops or archbishops.

As a result, one group of Catholics lost faith in the church. These people were so disgusted by Church corruption that they defied the priests, bishops, archbishops, and cardinals, and they refused to take oaths of allegiance to the pope. The Albigensians, as they were called since they lived near the city of Albi in the south of France, were in fact against any form of government. Innocent first sent his best missionaries, Bishop Diego of Osma and Dominic Guzmán (later St. Dominic), to reason with the Albigensians. The missionaries did not succeed; instead, the Albi rebellion spread across northern Italy.

Innocent was outraged. He called on the faithful in France to wage a crusade against the Albigensians: "Arise, Christian soldiers! The blood of the righteous cries to you to protect the Church against its enemies with the shield of faith. Arise and gird on your swords!" (Gontard, p. 260). One hundred thousand answered the call. The city of Béziers was the first to be attacked. By the time the town surrendered, in July 1209, the crusaders were in a mad frenzy—the city was destroyed and a reported twenty thousand of its citizens murdered.

The Children's Crusade. Innocent used the threat of more crusades to consolidate his power in Europe. One by one, the kings agreed to pay tribute to the pope and to accept his rule as law. Innocent claimed the right to crown the kings of Bulgaria, Bohemia, and Armenia. The kings of Hungary, Poland, Denmark, and England also agreed to his rule. Innocent was gaining power in the north and east.

In France, crusading became popular among the young. Stephen, a twelve-year-old boy, took up the call to free the Holy Land from Islamic occupation. He was joined by Nicholas, who called upon German youth to march with them. In 1212 thousands of youths joined in a march toward Jerusalem. They planned to take ships from Marseilles in France and from Genoa in Italy. Innocent was shocked; he called for the children to go home, but thousands milled around Europe for a time. Most of them finally did return home but a few were joined by priests and set sail from Marseilles. These few were not heard from again for thirty years. Finally, word came that the children had been sold into slavery in Africa. The Children's Crusade, as it came to be known, unsettled Innocent but did not turn him against crusading.

Francis of Agassi. Two years after the Children's Crusade, Innocent was faced with a new challenge. A small, shabbily dressed visitor asked to see the pope. His name was Francis, he said, and he wanted to start a new order of priests. They would live a life of poverty as had Jesus Christ. These disciples would

bring back the purity of the original Church by giving up all worldly goods, teaching Christian ideas, and asking only for enough food and clothes to meet basic needs. At first the pope rejected the proposal, but Francis persisted until Innocent agreed to test the idea.

Planning the Fifth Crusade. Innocent was now in his fifties and in ill health. Still, he did not relax his efforts to build one Christian world united under the laws of the Church. Major obstacles, however, remained in his path. In 1211, for example, a group of Muslims had declared war on Christianity and began the invasion of Spain.

By 1215 Innocent had devised a new plan and called for a meeting of Church authorities. The Lateran Council met on November 11, 1215, with more than 2,200 leaders from three continents gathered to hear the pope's words. Present were 70 cardinals, 412 bishops, 900 abbots and priors, representatives of all the major Catholic governments, and the Knights of the Order of Chivalry. They listened to the pope call for purifying the Church through reform, but mostly they heard a call for a Fifth Crusade. Four earlier ones had failed to free the Holy Land, but Innocent was ready for a new attempt.

Innocent told the leaders at the council that kings would provide the necessary troops. In addition, money for the crusade would be easier to get this time because he would tax the wealthy officials of the Church. (In spite of Innocent's guard against it, the priests and bishops of the Church had often become wealthy.) One of the strongest leaders stepped forward to spearhead the crusade, Frederick II, King of the Germans.

Two other actions were approved by this council. Francis of Agassi and Dominic Guzmán were given permission to form new groups of Catholic priests. They were to spread Christianity around the world. Francis's group would teach by example, living a life of poverty and unconditional compassion. Dominic would

◄
The Lateran Council; the 2,200 leaders present heard a call for a Fifth Crusade.

form a preaching order of missionaries. As a result of these efforts, Christianity spread more rapidly through the world. The two men later became St. Francis of Assisi and St. Dominic. Their priestly orders endured as the Franciscans and Dominicans.

The death of Innocent III. By 1216, the middle of the next year, Innocent was again on the road, traveling north to pass judgment on a squabble between two cities. On the way, he developed a fever. He died on the return trip in the city of Perugia, on July 16, 1216. He had not seen his last crusade begin.

Aftermath

The Sixth Crusade. Frederick II did not prove effective as a mobilizer of resources, and the Fifth Crusade became in danger of faltering. Meanwhile, Francis of Assisi made his own pilgrimage to Jerusalem and spoke with the Muslim leaders there. He persuaded them to let him roam freely through the city, though he did not persuade them to turn to Christianity.

At the same time, the new pope, who called himself Gregory IX, swore to carry out Innocent's work. Upset by the delays of the Fifth Crusade, Gregory excommunicated Frederick II. In order to get back into the Church, Frederick organized another, the sixth, crusade, and in the late 1220s, he led his armies toward Jerusalem. Reaching the city, he bargained with the old Muslim leader who had defended Jerusalem in the past. The two agreed to let Christians rule Jerusalem. The world of God under the pope was finally gaining a foothold in the Middle East.

Genghis Khan. The man "sent of Heaven," however, was moving west. Genghis Khan had captured Beijing (Peking) in 1215, the year of the call for the Fifth Crusade. He had taken nearly all of China under his rule and moved on to Russia and beyond. As his troops marched deeper into Europe, the kings of eastern Europe became afraid and called on the pope to rescue them from the Mongols. But Gregory did little more than correspond with the Mongol leadership. Frederick II had returned from Jerusalem to find his own power threatened by the pope. Frederick might have helped eastern Europe defend against the

Mongols, but his army was marching toward Rome to challenge the pope.

The Hungarians in eastern Europe were left to defend their country alone. By 1223 Genghis Khan's army was moving in rapidly, and Bela of Hungary was preparing for a last defense. Just as the invasion of Europe was beginning, however, Genghis Khan changed his plan. His army's supply line had grown too long, and so he was forced to turn back toward Asia.

For More Information

Gontard, Friedrich. *The Chair of Peter: A History of the Papacy.* New York: Holt, Rinehart and Winston, 1964.

Walsh, Michael J. *An Illustrated History of the Popes: St. Peter to John Paul.* New York: St. Martin's, 1980.

Wiedenfeld, G., and R. Nicholson. *The Papacy: An Illustrated History from St. Peter to Paul VI.* Boston: Houghton Mifflin, 1964.

Alexius V

d. 1204

Personal Background

Young politician. Alexius Ducas was a local politician in Constantinople, the capital of the Byzantine Empire, at the beginning of the thirteenth century. His nickname was Murtzuphlus, a term that referred to his bushy eyebrows, which met above the bridge of his nose. Murtzuphlus evidently did not come from a prominent family. Although he is reported to have had some relationship to a well-off family named Angeli, there are no records of his early life.

Soldier and speaker. In adulthood, Murtzuphlus was a capable soldier and a good speaker. He became a leader of the people, able to rally the citizens of Constantinople with his fiery speeches and determination. At that time, Constantinople had been in a state of decline for more than one hundred years. It had suffered a powerful blow a century earlier when conquest-seeking Turks forced the emperor and defender of the Greek Orthodox Church, Alexius I, to ask for help from Pope Urban II in Rome. Urban had sent so many soldiers, in what would become known as the First Crusade, that the emperor did not know how to mamage them. Many of the crusaders stayed to make a living in the then-rich city. Constantinople's population became mixed, with Roman crusaders, Greek Orthodox citizens, and Muslims maintaining an uneasy peace and prospering from the city's position as a major center of trade.

▲ **In Alexius V's time, Constantinople's popula-tion was mixed.**

Event: The fall of Constantinople to the crusaders.

Role: A politician known for his support of the Greek Orthodox Church, Alexius V stormed the palace at Constantinople and deposed the Byzantine emperor who had been installed by the crusaders. The last of the eastern emperors of Byzantium, he was unable to hold off the crusaders, who sacked Constantinople and divided the Byzantine Empire among themselves and their supporters.

Greek champion. In this cosmopolitan city, Murtzuphlus aligned himself with the Greek Orthodox population. He was, however, always on the lookout for ways to extend his power. In 1201 he decided to strengthen the position of the Greeks and himself by taking over the government. A man called Alexius III had taken the throne by force, and Murtzuphlus led a palace revolution to overthrow him. Although the attempt failed, it convinced the emperor of Murtzuphlus's ability to rally the citizens. In order to win him over and thus eliminate him as a threat, Alexius III gave Murtzuphlus his daughter in marriage.

In those times it was customary for kings to express friendship and seal a treaty by arranging marriages for their daughters and sons. In fact, Eudocia, the daughter whom Alexius III had married to Murtzuphlus, had been married before to seal another agreement. Her husband from that arrangement, Stephen I of Serbia, had divorced Eudocia just a year earlier. Eudocia's marriage to Murtzuphlus revealed just how threatening the emperor believed Murtzuphlus and his anti-Roman group to be.

Murtzuphlus's Constantinople. As the capital of the Byzantine Empire, which separated Europe from Asia and the Middle East, Constantinople was at the crossroads of Eastern and Western cultures. Because of its location at this nexus, the city had become an important trade center and perhaps the richest metropolis in the world.

The Byzantines were descendants of the ancient Greeks, and though they were Christians, they did not recognize the authority of the Roman pope. Little more than one hundred years before Murtzuphlus's time, Turkish invaders had begun to move into parts of the Byzantine Empire. When the emperor, in the late eleventh century, asked Pope Urban II for military help to drive

Cast of Characters

The Byzantine Empire in the early thirteenth century was marked by enough intrigue to fill the pages of a mystery book. This is the cast of major characters in the drama:

Isaac: A previous emperor of Constantinople.

Alexius III: Brother of Isaac, who took his brother prisoner and put his eyes out.

Alexius IV: Son of Isaac, who allied himself with the crusaders to regain the throne for Isaac and himself.

Alexius V (Murtzuphlus): Champion of the Greeks against the Roman crusaders.

Enrique Dandolo: The aged ruler of Venice, a leader of the crusaders, who hated the Greeks for mistreating him when he visited Constantinople in 1171.

out the Turks, he promised, in return, to allow the pope greater authority over the Greek Orthodox Church (the Byzantine Christian Church). This set in motion the Crusades, during which successive generations of western Europeans traveled far from home for the declared purpose of freeing the Holy Land (Palestine) from the Islamic rule of the Turks and other Muslim leaders.

Unfortunately, Urban II's First Crusade overwhelmed Constantinople with Roman, or Latin, crusaders. The cultural differences between the Byzantine descendants of Greece and the Latins made the alliance an uneasy one. The Byzantines, who were richer and more experienced with varied cultures, considered the Latins vulgar and barbaric, while the Latins thought the Arabic influence on the Byzantine culture less Christian and thus less trustworthy. Still, beyond the occasional street brawl, the residents of Constantinople felt they had little to fear from the Latins. But one day in the summer of 1202, they were proven wrong.

Innocent III and Enrique Dandolo. Innocent III (see entry) had called for a Fourth Crusade to recapture Jerusalem from the Muslims. Thousands of soldiers gathered to answer his call and headed east. They arrived at the seaport of Venice, Italy, to sail to the Middle East, but they did not have enough money to hire ships to transport them across the Adriatic Sea. The extremely wealthy ruler of Venice, Enrique Dandolo, saw an opportunity to acquire a trading city on the other side of this sea. He allowed the crusaders to make camp on an island he owned, but then threatened not to provide them with ships and to let them starve unless the crusaders agreed to a side trip. They would have to capture a city on the eastern side of the Adriatic for him. The desperate crusaders agreed. The city was Constantinople.

The other Alexius. Constantinople was then in the hands of Alexius III, who had taken the throne from his incapable and unpopular brother Isaac II. Isaac, blinded by his brother, had been helped out of prison by his son, Alexius IV. Alexius IV and Isaac met with the crusaders before their arrival in Constantinople and asked their help in restoring Isaac to the throne. Dandolo, who had accompanied the crusaders on their mission to capture Constantinople for him, hated the Byzantines. He had been

Venice's ambassador to Constantinople thirty years earlier and had been mistreated. Dandolo readily agreed to Isaac's request to overthrow the Byzantine government.

On June 24, 1203, the fleet of crusaders appeared off the shores of Constantinople, prepared for battle. With them were Alexius IV and Isaac. The leaders of this fleet demanded that Isaac be restored to the throne and that Alexius IV join him as co-emperor. Knowing that Constantinople was not prepared to fight, the citizens reluctantly submitted. Alexius III escaped to claim a small part of the empire elsewhere, and Alexius IV and Isaac became rulers. Meanwhile, Murtzuphlus (Alexius V) had been watching all this intrigue, his hatred of the Latin crusaders growing.

Participation:
The Fall of Constantinople to the Crusaders

Riots. The new arrangement was totally unacceptable to Murtzuphlus, who realized that the new emperors were merely puppets for the Latins. Pretending to support Alexius IV, he gained the new emperor's trust and a government position. Immediately, however, Murtzuphlus began working to overthrow the government. Unknown to the emperors, he proclaimed himself the leader of an antigovernment movement and organized riots in the streets of Constantinople. One of these riots, in January 1204, resulted in the destruction of the great statue of Athena—a priceless ancient sculpture that long before had been imported from the Acropolis in Athens.

The riots demonstrated the citizens' unhappiness with Alexius IV and revealed the popularity of Murtzuphlus. It also showed how powerless the emperors would be without the support of the Latin crusaders, who remained camped outside the city walls waiting for Alexius IV to fulfill his part of their bargain: they demanded payment promised them for their role in restoring Isaac to the throne of Byzantium, part of which included passage to Egypt, where they would pursue their original mission to free holy sites from Muslim control.

Murtzuphlus, the new emperor. But the government of the Byzantine Empire was low on funds, and Alexius IV could not

▲ Crusaders disembarking in Egypt; to win Dandolo's support, Alexius IV promised to provide the crusaders with transportation to Egypt.

satisfy the crusaders' demands. Moreover, the people of Constantinople were growing increasingly unhappy, and Alexius IV suspected that he and Isaac would soon be removed from power. Still believing Murtzuphlus to be loyal, the emperor sent him to the crusaders with a request for protection from his own people. Murtzuphlus left the palace with no intention of meeting the Latins. Instead, he quickly organized a mob and returned to overthrow Alexius IV.

Because Alexius IV was so unpopular, Murtzuphlus met with no resistance at the palace. He had Alexius IV thrown into a dungeon and strangled, and late in January 1204, he proclaimed himself Emperor Alexius V. Isaac disappeared, presumably killed by the new emperor.

Murtzuphlus was brave but foolish. He denied responsibility for every agreement the former emperor had made with the Latins and ordered the crusaders away from Constantinople. Realizing his actions would cause the crusaders to attack, he began immediate fortification of the city.

The attack. The crusaders did not attack for several months, and Murtzuphlus began to suspect that his own government was plotting against him. He dismissed every minister whom he suspected of disloyalty and demanded such dictatorial military discipline that even his once loyal followers began to disagree with his management. Meanwhile, outside the fortified walls of Constantinople, the crusaders were busy dividing the spoils of the city in advance. Dandolo and his Venetians would take three-eighths of the wealth of the empire; the crusaders would take another three-eighths. The rest would be left to the crusade-appointed emperors.

The first offensive of the combined Venetian-crusader force came one dawn in early April, by sea. Murtzuphlus set up headquarters on a hilltop, giving him a view of the engaging fleets, and personally took charge of his troops. The Venetians brought their ships as close as possible to the steep city walls, hoping that the crusaders would be able to leap onto the walls and open the city gates. Murtzuphlus's soldiers on the walls drove off attack after attack. At mid-afternoon, Dandolo, also personally leading his forces, called off the attack. Nonetheless Byzantine losses were so great that the people within the city began to wonder about their leadership.

The fall of Constantinople. On April 13, 1204, the attack resumed, but this time with twice as many crusader ships carrying twice as many men. The Byzantine guards were able to keep the Venetian fleet away until noon. Then, when an unexpected gust of wind blew the ships so close to shore that crusaders were able to jump from them onto the city walls. Shortly thereafter, they were able to fight their way to the gates and open them. Latins poured into the city on horseback. Chaos followed.

Escape. Murtzuphlus retreated to his palace. That night, he and Eudocia fled Constantinople along with thousands of other refugees. They went to Mosynopolis, in Thrace, where Alexius III—the man whose government Murtzuphlus had tried to overthrow in 1201—was living in exile. Murtzuphlus hoped to join the other evicted emperor and with him try to regain Constantinople.

Aftermath

The sacking of the city. Constantinople fell completely to the Latins within days of the attack, and the crusaders were allowed three days of pillaging. Never had these men seen such wealth, and the idea of moving on to the Holy Land was completely forgotten. The carnage that followed was marked in history for its ruthlessness and utter disregard for all things sacred. After that, any ideas of reuniting the Greek Orthodox Church with Rome were completely abandoned.

Blindness and death. While Murtzuphlus may have been spared the sight of Constantinople's plunder, his own fate was no better. He received no pity from his father-in-law in Mosynopolis; Alexius III found another husband for his daughter Eudocia and had Murtzuphlus blinded. Nevertheless, Murtzuphlus was able to evade capture for almost a year, until a French knight caught him by surprise and arrested him. Murtzuphlus was brought back to Constantinople, where he was forced to climb a great sculptured column and jump to his death. It was considered a fitting end for Murtzuphlus, taking into account both his rank and his treachery.

For More Information

Armstrong, Karen. *Holy War: The Crusades and Their Impact on Today's World.* Garden City, New York: Doubleday, 1991.

Bradford, Ernie. *The Sword and the Scimitar: The Saga of the Crusades.* Milan, Italy: G. P. Putnam's Sons, 1974.

Franzius, Enno. *History of the Byzantine Empire.* New York: Funk & Wagnalls, 1967.

Robinson, John L. *Dungeon, Fire and Sword: The Knights Templar in the Crusades.* New York: M. Evans, 1991.

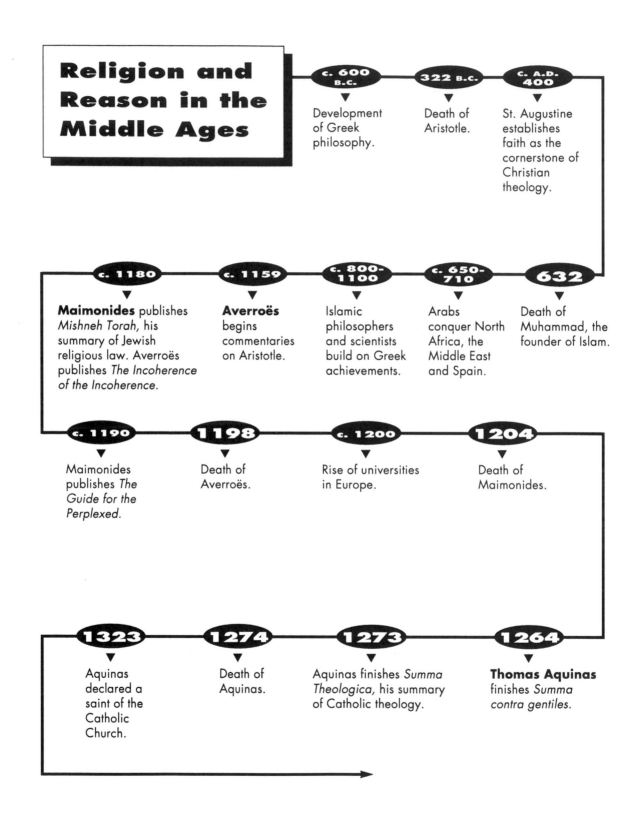

Religion and Reason in the Middle Ages

c. 600 B.C.
Development of Greek philosophy.

322 B.C.
Death of Aristotle.

c. A.D. 400
St. Augustine establishes faith as the cornerstone of Christian theology.

c. 1180
Maimonides publishes *Mishneh Torah,* his summary of Jewish religious law. Averroës publishes *The Incoherence of the Incoherence.*

c. 1159
Averroës begins commentaries on Aristotle.

c. 800–1100
Islamic philosophers and scientists build on Greek achievements.

c. 650–710
Arabs conquer North Africa, the Middle East and Spain.

632
Death of Muhammad, the founder of Islam.

c. 1190
Maimonides publishes *The Guide for the Perplexed.*

1198
Death of Averroës.

c. 1200
Rise of universities in Europe.

1204
Death of Maimonides.

1323
Aquinas declared a saint of the Catholic Church.

1274
Death of Aquinas.

1273
Aquinas finishes *Summa Theologica,* his summary of Catholic theology.

1264
Thomas Aquinas finishes *Summa contra gentiles.*

RELIGION AND REASON IN THE MIDDLE AGES

Out of the classical world of the Roman Empire grew the Middle Ages, shaped by the appearance of new peoples and religions. In Western Europe, the empire's old heartland, barbarian tribes from the north settled in France, Germany, Spain, and Italy, mixing with earlier inhabitants to produce the peoples of today's Europe. In the Middle East, North Africa, and Spain, Arabs conquered huge tracts of territory, also blending with earlier inhabitants to form a new, Arab-based culture.

These Western and Eastern cultures shared common elements, which they had inherited from Roman times. From the Jews, an ancient people who had lived uneasily under Roman rule, came a powerful religious concept called monotheism, the belief in a single God, an all-powerful Creator. Jewish traditions gave rise to both Christianity, the religion of Europe in the Middle Ages, and Islam, the religion of the Arab world.

The Middle Ages also inherited another powerful influence from the ancient world: the philosophy of classical Greece, including a vast body of scientific writings. But Greek philosophy was very complex—and it had been recorded in Greek, which was not spoken or read as widely as in the past. In the West, Latin took over as the language of learning, while Arabic dominated the Islamic world. The Arabs, however, had conquered lands in which the Greek works were still read by the native peoples, either in Greek or in native languages such as Syrian. Greek writings therefore filtered first into the Islamic world, helping to create a golden age of Islamic learning, of science and philosophy based on Greek models. And the greatest model of them all was the work of Aristotle, the philosopher whose writings addressed virtually every area of knowledge and praised human reason above all else.

Many Islamic scholars contributed to this golden age, as did many Jewish scholars living in Islamic lands. Like later Christian scholars, however, they faced great difficulty as they tried to reconcile Greek philosophy with their own beliefs. The basic ideas underlying their religions and the basic ideas underlying Greek philosophy seemed at odds with each other. Islam, Judaism, and Christianity are based on faith; Greek philosophy, on reason. How, then, could these religions address the vast body of Greek philosophy? How, especially, could they incorporate the ideas of Aristotle, the master of reason, whose thoughtful, comprehensive writings could not be ignored?

In the Islamic world, this process of reconciling philosophy and religion reached its climax with the twelfth-century Spanish-Arab philosopher **Averroës.** Building on the work of earlier Islamic philosophers, especially the Persian Avicenna, Averroës devoted his life to explaining Aristotle's work in a way that dovetailed with his Muslim (Islamic) beliefs. Much of his writing took the form of commentary, or essays summarizing Aristotle's work and ideas. Ultimately, Averroës took the position that faith and reason are separate but equal ways of approach-

Monotheism Versus Greek Philosophy

Each of the three monotheistic religions has a body of holy writings that provides the basis for its doctrines, or official beliefs. Jews have the Hebrew scriptures, comprised of the Torah, the prophets' works, and other sacred writings; Christians have the Bible, which includes the Hebrew Scriptures, as well as the New Testament; and Muslims have the Koran. These holy books "reveal" the truth to believers—but the believers must trust in the books completely. What the holy books tell them about God cannot be proven by reason: believers must have faith.

By contrast, Greek philosophy as a whole, is based upon reason. Aristotle made rational thought part of a system that he called logic, which calls for the weighing of evidence and proof in determining what is true. On the surface at least, Aristotle seems to be the enemy of faith.

ing life's truths. His ideas, however, were rejected by many Muslim religious authorities, who felt faith was more important.

The Jewish philosopher **Maimonides** lived at about the same time as Averroës. He was also born in the same city, Cordoba, Spain, though he spent most of his life in Egypt. Like Averroës, Maimonides wrote commentaries on Aristotle's work. He combined Aristotle's ideas with Jewish values in his most famous work, *The Guide for the Perplexed*. Unlike Averroës, however, Maimonides argued that faith and reason were deeply connected. Reason, he said, was the path to true faith.

In the following century, the Christian theologian and philosopher **Thomas Aquinas** combined elements of Averroës and Maimonides's approaches to formulate his own solution to the problem. For Aquinas, faith and reason could explain different aspects of God's existence and nature. God's existence, Aquinas believed, could be proven using reason; God's nature, on the other hand, could only be accepted on faith. Though Aquinas's views won little acceptance during his lifetime, soon after his death in 1274 they were officially adopted by the Catholic Church. Aquinas was declared a saint in 1323.

Averroës

1126-1198

Personal Background

The man known in the Christian West as Averroës was born in Cordoba, the capital of Spain under Muslim rule. His full name in Arabic shows his ancestry: Abu al-Walid Muhammad ibn Ahmad ibn Muhammad ibn Rushd, or "Abu al-Walid Muhammad, the son of Ahmad, the son of Muhammad, the son of Rushd" ("ibn" means "son of" in Arabic). Because his grandfather, had exactly the same name, Averroës was also called al-Hafid, "the grandson." Averroës was born in 1126, the same year his grandfather died.

Qadi. Averroës's grandfather was a leading *qadi,* or religious judge, a man highly trained in the religious laws that governed Islamic society. These laws were based on the teachings of the Prophet Muhammad, who had lived nearly six centuries earlier in Arabia. It was the qadi's job to help interpret Islamic doctrine, to decide how it should be applied in making and carrying out laws. Like his grandfather, Averroës' father was also a qadi. Not surprisingly, Averroës received a very complete education in Islamic law.

Science, philosophy, and Aristotle. Averroës also studied with masters of science, medicine, and philosophy, famous teachers of the day whose work was an important part of Moorish culture's overall strength (see box). One of them, a teacher of medi-

▲ Averroës

Event: Religion and reason meet in Islamic thought.

Role: In his "commentaries," or essays, on the work of the ancient Greek philosopher Aristotle, Averroës tried to reconcile Islamic beliefs with the ideas of Greek philosophy. Although his writings never found acceptance in the Islamic world, they deeply influenced Christian philosophers, such as Thomas Aquinas, who wrestled with similar issues.

cine, introduced Averroës to the writings of Aristotle. The ancient Greek philosopher's ideas covered every branch of learning. Aristotle's work gripped Averroës with excitement. It would eventually occupy a central place in his life. In turn, Averroës would give Aristotle's ideas renewal, helping to spread the great philosopher's work to new audiences during the Middle Ages.

Participation: Religion and Reason Meet in Islamic Philosophy

Astronomy in Morocco. In 1153, when he was twenty-seven, Averroës spent time in the city of Marrakesh, in Morocco. There he made detailed observations of the stars, comparing what he saw with what Aristotle and others had written about the heavens. In Morocco, close to the deserts of North Africa, skies were clearer than in Al-Andalus (Spain), and Averroës could observe stars not visible at home. He could also use the distance between Al-Andalus and Morocco to compare the different positions of a star in the sky. He even discovered a star that had never before been noticed. (That was a bit of beginner's luck, for in the days before telescopes most visible stars had been named centuries earlier.) A few years later, in 1159, Averroës used what he had learned to write a commentary, or explanatory essay, on Aristotle's astronomy book *On the Heavens*.

Introduction to the sultan. Though Averroës was never more than an amateur astronomer (his other interests soon took over), the most famous story about him concerns his knowledge of the stars. One of his friends was Ibn Tufayl, an elderly philosopher who was also the personal doctor of the sultan (ruler). Ibn Tufayl wanted Averroës to meet

Moorish Spain

Soon after Muhammad's death in the year 632, Muslim Arabs conquered North Africa, spreading their new religion from Egypt to Morocco. They then had crossed into Europe, occupying Spain, which they called Al-Andalus. The resulting culture, called Moorish, was a lively blend of Arabic, North African, and Spanish influences. Though Jewish and Christian communities also played an important role, Moorish society was strictly governed by Islamic religious beliefs. By Averroës's time, however, Christian kingdoms in Portugal and northern Spain had begun to drive the Muslims out of the Spanish peninsula. This long process, called the "Reconquest," ended in 1492, when the last Muslim territory fell to the Christian rulers Ferdinand and Isabella.

the sultan and managed to arrange an introduction. It was the same year that Averroës was writing his commentary on *On the Heavens*. As he introduced his younger friend, Ibn Tufayl told the sultan about Averroës's great knowledge of philosophy, his wide learning, and his piercing intelligence. The sultan looked at Averroës. "What," he asked, "is the opinion of the philosophers on the skies? Are they made of eternal substance or did they have a beginning?" (Urvoy, p. 32).

Faced with such a question from the ruler of Islamic Spain, Averroës froze. However, the sultan himself came to the rescue, resuming the conversation by asking Ibn Tufayl about the views of different philosophers. Averroës then relaxed and joined in the discussion, but the story of his temporary speechlessness became popular—especially after he had won a reputation for wisdom.

Mission. It was about that time that Ibn Tufayl gave Averroës a mission. "Would to God," Ibn Tufayl exclaimed to his friend, "that we could find someone willing to make a commentary upon [the] works [of Aristotle] and explain their meaning clearly so as to render them accessible to men!" (Urvoy, p. 32). He himself was too old to undertake such a large job, Ibn Tufayl continued, but a young man like Averroës would be perfect for it. And so Averroës took it on. It would occupy him for the rest of his life, as he struggled to bring Aristotle's ideas to a larger audience. Aristotle's writings had often been translated from Greek into other languages and then translated again into Arabic. Each translation was like an added filter that made it harder to grasp the original meaning. And beyond the language problem, of course, was the difficulty of the ideas themselves.

Of Greeks. Since Islam's early days, Muslim thinkers had struggled to grasp the nature of their religious faith and to under-

> ### *Falsafah*
>
> Aristotle had long been familiar to Islamic thinkers, who recognized him as the greatest authority in *falsafah*—the Arabic word for "philosophy." The ancient Greeks' wide-ranging ideas formed the basis for the Muslims' own progress in science and medicine, which the Muslims (like the Greeks) came to consider part of philosophy. Ibn Sina (980-1037), called Avicenna in the West was an early Muslim philosopher. A Persian, Avicenna relied heavily on Aristotle's writings. Such writings had found their way into Muslim hands mostly through the Greeks and other Christians whom the Arabs had conquered.

▲ Aristotle; Averroës was, in effect, assigned to explain Aristotle's philosophy in a way that made sense to faithful Muslims.

stand how it related to what can actually be known and understood about the world. What kind of knowledge was more valid, they wondered, the knowledge of God that one attains through faith, or the kind of knowledge that comes through observation and study? Like the Christians who had pondered the same questions, Muslim writers such as Avicenna (Ibn Sina) and Averroës naturally turned to the ancient Greeks for answers to these and other questions.

Gaps. Greek philosophy offered systems of thought (such as logic) that can serve as tools for answering such questions.

And of all the Greeks, Aristotle had the most to say about logic, reason, and other modes of human understanding. In fact, Aristotle had written about so many subjects that the very range of his writings gave readers a feeling of great confidence in reason, in man's ability to understand the world. One subject he did not address, however, was faith. Faith was not part of Greek philosophy. The ideas of Aristotle and the other ancients had to be adapted to fit with the ideas of newer cultures such as Islam. The assignment that Ibn Tufayl had given Averroës was, in effect, to explain Aristotle in a way that made sense to faithful Muslims.

Avicenna and al-Ghazali. Luckily for him, Averroës had the work of past Muslim philosophers to use as a starting point. In fact, the debate about faith and reason had been going on for some time in Islamic society. One of reason's supporters had been Avicenna, a scientist and philosopher. His complicated philosophy had joined reason and faith, praising faith while putting more emphasis on reason. Avicenna had suggested that faith was somehow based on reason. It was important to practice and believe according to one's religion, Avicenna argued, but to do so with a clear understanding of nature. That understanding must be based on science and philosophy.

Faith Versus Reason

The ancient Greek philosophers lived long before the rise of Christianity and Islam. Their ideas did not always fit in easily with the belief in a single God, an all-powerful Creator. Such a belief (which both Christians and Muslims had taken from much older Jewish traditions) seemed to rest on faith, an acceptance of something that could never actually be proven. Faith clearly played a role in questions addressed by the ancient philosophers, questions such as the nature of good and evil, for example. Yet the Greeks supported man's ability to understand such ideas with arguments and proofs. Called reason, these deductions seemed to go against the idea of faith, so important to Christians, Jews, and Muslims.

Avicenna's ideas had been opposed by another Muslim philosopher, al-Ghazali (1058-1111). Rejecting the important role that Avicenna had given to reason, al-Ghazali argued that faith alone should be sufficient to answer all questions. One shouldn't try to understand nature, he claimed; one should just accept it as God's creation. Al-Ghazali's best-known book was *The Incoherence of the Philosophers*. As the title suggests, in it al-Ghazali attacks the ideas of Avicenna and others who built upon the work of the Greek philosophers.

The Incoherence of the Incoherence. Averroës wrote his own most famous book in response to al-Ghazali. Called *The Incoherence of the Incoherence,* its title was a joking attack on al-Ghazali's title. In it, Averroës takes the position that both faith and reason have a place, but that they are distinctly separate from each other. Neither, he wrote, is based on the other. Both are equal, and if they are practiced correctly, they will usually agree. Getting faith and reason to agree, however, meant taking a more relaxed view of religion than some found acceptable.

Almohads. *The Incoherence* was published around 1180, when Averroës was in his fifties. Up to then, he had been writing steadily, having completed more than thirty commentaries explaining the works of Aristotle, as well as works on medicine, astronomy, and physics. Like his father and grandfather, he had also had a career as an important public official, serving as a qadi in Seville and Cordoba.

During Averroës's lifetime, major changes took place in the Moorish world. In the days of his grandfather, Moorish rulers had been members of the Almoravid dynasty. Now, however, power had passed to the Almohads, strict religious reformers from North Africa. The sultan to whom Ibn Tufayl had introduced Averroës was the third Almohad ruler. In 1182 Averroës succeeded Ibn Tufayl as the sultan's personal doctor. A few months later, he also became Grand Qadi of Cordoba, the city's chief religious judge. When the sultan's younger brother al-Mansur became sultan in 1184, Averroës retained his link to the court.

Disgrace and exile. In 1195, however, Averroës began to fall out of favor. Now almost seventy, he had enjoyed the friendship of the sultan for more than a decade. Yet there were pressures on the sultan. Almohad rule had not yet been accepted by all in Al-Andalus, and for the sultan, staying in power meant maintaining strict religious policies. It was their religious fundamentalism that had allowed the Almohads to come to power in the first place.

Now the sultan found his rule threatened by extremist religious uprisings, and he had to do something to keep the people happy. One of the things he decided to do was to banish his old friend Averroës, whose presence at the court had angered the fundamentalists. Averroës's beliefs were declared heretical (contrary to Islam), and his books burned. He was exiled to the small town of Lucena, near Cordoba. In the Jewish community there, so one story goes, Averroës and the great Jewish philosopher **Maimonides** (see entry), another interpreter of Aristotle, met and became friends. Though the story is probably false, the two philosophers did have much in common.

Aftermath

Return. In 1198, having transferred his capital to Marrakesh, in Morocco, the sultan sent for his old friend. Averroës went to Marrakesh but died a few months later. His body was brought back to his beloved Al-Andalus. Part of the trip was made by mule, and it was said that the weight of Averroës's body was balanced by a load of his own philosophy books—those that had escaped burning. Most of his surviving works were those that were translated into Hebrew or Latin, and had thus reached the hands of scholars such as Maimonides and **Thomas Aquinas** (see entry).

By the Book

One thing common to Jews, Christians, and Muslims is their reliance on a sacred book as a source of divine wisdom. Muslims take their beliefs from the Koran, which they consider the word of God as written down by the prophet Muhammad. In all of these faiths, fundamentalism usually means "going by the book"—in other words, taking the words literally and rejecting complicated interpretations that might leave room to deviate from the religious text as written. Averroës's relatively relaxed ideas about the Koran earned him the disfavor of the sultan.

For More Information

Holt, P. M., and others, editors. *Islamic Society and Civilization. The Cambridge History of Islam,* Vol. 2B. New York: Cambridge University Press, 1970.

Urvoy, Domenique. *Ibn Rushd (Averroës).* Translated by Olivia Stewart. London and New York: Routledge, 1991.

Maimonides

1135-1204

Personal Background

Moses ben Maimon, called Maimonides, was born in Cordoba, the capital of Islamic Spain. He came from a family of rabbis (Jewish religious leaders), one of whose ancestors, according to tradition, was the biblical King David. His father, Rabbi Maimon, had had a dream in which God told him to marry the daughter of a local butcher. He did so, and Maimonides was the result of that union.

Prodigal student. Maimonides' mother died giving birth to him. Though Maimon remarried and had other children, he had high expectations for his eldest son. He hoped Maimonides would follow him into the life of a rabbi. Young Maimonides himself, however, seemed to have no liking for the difficult studies such a life required. Maimon, the story goes, feared that Maimonides took after his mother, the uneducated butcher's daughter. He said as much to his son, demanding once again that Maimonides work at his studies. Instead, Maimonides left home.

It was not until some time later that the Jews of Cordoba were impressed by a mysterious young speaker who was giving a lecture at the main synagogue. Whoever it was had obviously spent long hours studying the ancient laws and traditions of the Jews. Only at the end of the speech did the boy remove the prayer shawl covering his face. Maimonides had returned, like the bibli-

▲ **Maimonides**

Event: Religion and reason meet in Jewish thought.

Role: The Jewish philosopher Maimonides inspired both respect and controversy in the medieval Jewish world with his wide-ranging summaries of Jewish law and tradition. Later, his *Guide for the Perplexed* deeply influenced Christian and Islamic thinkers as well. In it, Maimonides blended the philosophy of Aristotle with his own ideas about God, the Hebrew Scriptures, and other aspects of traditional Jewish teachings.

cal story of the prodigal son, to the house—and studies—of his father. He had spent his time away from home studying with the same rabbi who had taught Maimon himself years earlier.

Almohads. Soon after his return, Maimonides's family was forced to leave Cordoba. In earlier times, Muslims, Jews, and Christians had lived peacefully together under Islamic rule. About the time that Maimonides was born, however, the Almohads, strict religious reformers, were taking power in North Africa and Spain. Under these Muslim puritans, Jews and Christians no longer enjoyed a comfortable place in Islamic society. Many were killed, and others were forced to become Muslims—or at least to worship as Muslims publicly, while observing their own faiths in secret. Maimonides's family was among the Jewish refugees from Almohad rule. Maimonides was about thirteen when the Almohads conquered Cordoba and Maimon took his family to Almeria, in southwest Spain.

Participation:
Religion and Reason Meet in Jewish Thought

Mishnah. There Maimonides continued his education, studying philosophy and science as well as the religious writings on which Jewish culture is based. As a part of his studies, he began work on a commentary, or explanation, of the Talmud, the ancient writings that form the basis of Jewish law. In 1158 he decided to focus his efforts on the Mishnah, the first part of the Talmud. Over the centuries, he feared, it had grown so complicated that only those who devoted their lives to studying it could master its contents.

Though only twenty-three, in 1158 Maimonides decided to write a book explaining the Mishnah's contents in simple language. That way, Jews would be able to refer to their religion's central tenets without wading through the long and confusing text of the Talmud itself. Its fundamental principles thus made accessible to everyone, Jewish religion and culture would have a better chance of surviving in Moorish areas, despite the Almohads' attempts to make Jews convert to Islam.

▲ A Jewish synagogue; only at the end of his lecture on ancient Jewish law and tradition did Maimonides remove the prayer shawl covering his face.

Flight to Fez. Only a year later, however, the Almohads won control of Almeria as well. Christians fleeing the Almohads usually headed north, to the Christian kingdoms of northern Spain. But, like many other Jews, the Maimon family chose to stay in the

Islamic world. They fled to the Moroccan city of Fez, across the Mediterranean in North Africa. Fez was also under Almohad control, but it was farther away from the Spanish power center of the Almohad rulers. It also had a large Jewish community; Maimonides could easily find the books and other resources he would need to finish his Mishnah commentary. His father and younger brother, David, were happy to make the move in order to help. In fact, they often gave Maimonides assistance. It was almost a family project. His father's knowledge proved helpful when Maimonides had a question, and David gave him a hand with research and note-taking.

Questions of science and faith. As he worked on the commentary in the following years, Maimonides also wrote essays on other subjects. Though interested mainly in religious issues, he became more and more of a secular philosopher as well. In Maimonides's day, philosophy included science and medicine. Using the texts of ancient Greek philosophers such as Aristotle, he wrote on logic and metaphysics as well, branches of philosophy that address the mental and spiritual aspects of the world, respectively.

Jews in the Moorish World

Conquered by Muslims in the century following the death of Muhammad in 632, North Africa and Spain—the Moorish world—took a leading part in Islamic culture. In the ninth century, under tolerant Arab rulers, Jewish thinkers in Moorish lands made important contributions to Islam's golden age of science and literature. Beginning under the Almohads in the twelfth century, Spanish Jews started to migrate throughout the rest of the Islamic world, mostly congregating in the Middle East. Today, their descendants are called Sephardim. Together, they and the Ashkenazim, descendants of Jews from Christian Europe, make up the two dominant branches of Jewish culture.

Maimonides also took a public stand in the biggest controversy facing Jews living under the Almohads: how to treat the "secret Jews," who had outwardly accepted Islam in order to avoid trouble with the Almohad rulers (Heschel, p. 39). While some called for expelling them from the Jewish community, Maimonides argued that they should not be blamed for giving in to pressure. In their homes and their hearts, they still observed Jewish laws and beliefs. That should be enough, he wrote. He supported his argument with passages from the Scriptures in which God forgives those who commit far worse sins yet still honor Him in the end. Ahab, King of Israel, for example, denied God for years but is

▲ **Maimonides fleeing to the Holy Land from Fez; in the 1160s anti-Jewish feeling in the Moorish world reached new heights.**

forgiven because he repented and fasted in God's name (1 Kings 21:27).

Journey to the Holy Land. In 1163, after five years in Fez, Maimonides and his family were again forced to move on. A new

Almohad ruler had come to power, and anti-Jewish feeling in the Moorish world reached new heights. They went first to Palestine, the Holy Land of the Bible, which was under the control of Christian crusaders from Europe. Few Jews remained there, even in Jerusalem, the holiest of places in Jewish history. Like the Almohads, the crusaders had made life very hard for Jews in the areas they conquered.

Egypt. Leaving the crusader kingdoms, Maimonides, David, and their father went south to Egypt, returning to Islamic territory. In the Cairo-area city of Fostat, with its prosperous Jewish community, the wandering family finally found refuge from the Almohads in 1166. Egypt was under the control of the Fatimid dynasty and the famed Saladin, whose religious policies were relaxed compared to those of the Almohads. In Fostat, Maimonides would live out the rest of his life, marrying and having a son, Abraham, who would help him in his work.

Mishneh Torah. After finishing his Mishnah commentary in 1168, Maimonides took on an even larger job in which he continued the approach begun with the commentary. In the *Mishneh Torah* ("Second Law," also known as the "Strong Hand" in English), Maimonides took on the complex body of laws that had grown up around the Mishnah, organizing them into a single, unified system. One of the most influential works in Jewish history, the *Mishneh Torah* has been called a constitution for the Jews. By the time he finished it, around 1180, Maimonides's fame had spread throughout the Jewish world. Respect for his learning and judgment made his name familiar to Muslim and Christian rulers and scholars as well.

Death and change. Maimonides's father had died just a few months after their arrival in Egypt. Then, sometime in the late 1170s, word came that his beloved David had drowned at sea while on a sailing voyage. Grief-stricken, Maimonides reached a turning point in his life. He and his family had often been on the run. His parents had died, and now his brother had been taken from him. All around him he had seen fellow Jews killed and terrorized. Even in Egypt, where Jews were relatively safe, religious and political conflicts constantly threatened the Jewish community. In his forties, Maimonides was widely recognized as the leading Jewish thinker of his time, perhaps of all time. Yet now he began to question some of his earlier ideas, especially about philosophy. Always attracted to the writings of Aristotle, he read the philosopher's works again.

A new view of the world began to take shape in his mind, a view that no longer put people at the center of things, as he had always assumed they were. After all, the universe had seemed designed by God to suit the convenience of human beings. As he thought things over, though, Maimonides slowly came around to almost exactly the opposite view. Perhaps, he concluded, humankind exists to suit the convenience of the universe. In other words, people are only a tiny part of a much larger plan that only God can begin to understand.

By viewing his own grief as less important in the wider view of God's creation, Maimonides was able to control it and, in the end, overcome it completely.

The Guide for the Perplexed. This understanding of the world led Maimonides to write his most famous work of philosophy, its title usually translated as *The Guide for the Perplexed.* In his earlier writings, he had used his training in philosophy to illuminate basic ideas in the tangle of Jewish tradition. Now he applied some of Aristotle's ideas to the faith of the Jews. Aristotle had been a champion of organized information and logic. He had also believed in such nonphysical entities as the human soul, but his approach to understanding them was through logic. As Maimonides explained in the book, he believed that there had once been a key part of Jewish thought that was like that of Aristotle but that it had been lost when the Jews were exiled from the Holy Land centuries earlier. He believed that faith in God was a sort of destination that could be reached through reason. He finished the work in about 1190.

No white beard. Philosophy and reason had led Maimonides to a new understanding of God, just as they had led him

The Guide for the Perplexed

In his introduction to *The Guide for the Perplexed*, Maimonides says that he wants to "offer guidance to the man who is knowledgeable in religion ... and is flawless in faith and character, but who has also studied philosophy, knows its problems, and is attracted by human reason" (Maimonides in Heschel, p. 205).

to a new understanding of the world. In both cases, humankind had lost its central role. For just as the universe could be understood without putting human beings at the center of it, so too could an all-powerful creator not based on human attributes. In *The Guide for the Perplexed,* Maimonides rejected the traditional view of God as an old man with a white beard, or as having any kind of body or personality at all. Instead, God can be "seen" only with the eyes of reason and faith together. God "is" the world, and one way that God is revealed is through the laws that govern the world.

Thus, understanding those laws—the laws of science—is the best way to understand God's message. Only through this use of reason can true faith be attained. Maimonides view, however, was unpopular among more traditional Jews, who wished to take the Scriptures literally and think of God as a personality.

Aftermath

Controversy. *The Guide for the Perplexed* eventually had a stronger influence in the Christian world than in the Jewish one. Its blend of religious faith and Aristotelian reason influenced later thinkers like **Thomas Aquinas** (see entry) and Albertus Magnus. It was Maimonides's earlier works that assured him his place in Jewish culture. The "Thirteen Articles of Faith" from his Mishnah commentary have been used for centuries as a standard feature of Jewish prayer books. The *Mishneh Torah,* like the *Guide,* however, stirred controversy in the Jewish world. Some complained that Maimonides had not included the sources of the many laws and legal opinions he had summarized. Still, the work has stood as the most important collection of Jewish law outside of the Talmud itself.

Medicine and politics. In the last two decades of his life, Maimonides took a leading role in public life, occupying the position of *nagib,* or head of Egypt's Jewish community. He was also the personal doctor of Sultan Saladin, who had unified the Islamic world in resistance to the crusaders. And he kept writing, producing major works on medicine that built on the findings of Greek medical scholars like Galen and Hippocrates. Maimonides died in Fostat on December 13, 1204.

For More Information

Heschel, Abraham Joshua. *Maimonides*. 1935. Reprint, New York: Farrar, Straus & Giroux, 1982.

Yellin, David, and Israel Abrahams. *Maimonides*. Philadelphia: Jewish Publication Society of America, 1903.

Zeitlin, Solomon. *Maimonides*. Originally published in 1935. Reprint, New York: Bloch, 1955.

Thomas Aquinas

1225-1274

Personal Background

Tommaso d'Aquino, (Thomas Aquinas in English), was born in 1225 in his family's castle at Roccasecca, near Aquino, Italy, about halfway between Rome and Naples. The family was large and noble, if not very rich, for Aquinas's father was a count and his mother was descended from the French conquerors of southern Italy. Aquinas was the youngest son.

Monte Cassino. Aquinas's family must have had early hopes of a religious life for him, because when he was about five they put him in the care of monks at the nearby monastery of Monte Cassino. There, as an "oblate" (one who was "offered" to the monastic life), Aquinas was raised and educated. He learned Latin and spent hours reading the Bible, early Christian writers such as St. Augustine, and writings by Benedictine monks. The windswept, mountaintop monastery belonged to the Benedictine order, the West's oldest organization of monks, which was founded by St. Benedict in the sixth century. One of Aquinas's uncles had been abbot (head) of the monastery, and the family may have hoped that Aquinas would rise to the same position.

Conflict. Roccasecca lay along the border between two warring powers: the kingdom of Naples, under the control of the emperor Frederick II, and the pope, who ruled from Rome. (Aside from being head of the Catholic Church, in medieval times the

▲ **Thomas Aquinas**

Event: Religion and reason meet in Christian thought.

Role: Building on the works of earlier Christian, Islamic, and Jewish writers, Thomas Aquinas's writings join religious faith and reason in a Christian outlook. Aquinas's explanation of how faith and reason can exist together deeply influenced both the Catholic Church and Western philosophy.

pope was also one of Italy's many local rulers. His armies fought battles just like any other ruler's.) Aquinas's family, despite its Benedictine connections, was allied with the emperor, and his father and brothers served in the emperor's army. In 1239, when Aquinas was about fourteen, a battle took place between the two sides near the monastery. To escape the violence, Aquinas was sent to the University of Naples, which Frederick II had established about the time of Aquinas's birth.

Participation: Religion and Reason Meet in Christian Thought

Averroës and Aristotle. It was probably in Naples, at Frederick's exciting new university, that Aquinas first came into contact with the books that would shape his life's work. Naples was a thriving seaport, full of people from all over the Mediterranean. Frederick supported not only Christian scholars, but also Islamic and Jewish ones.

Western scholars first encountered many of Aristotle's writings in the works of the Islamic philosophers Avicenna and **Averroës** (see entry). These Muslims had written "commentaries" on many of Aristotle's books, essays explaining the Greek philosopher's complicated ideas. Another philosopher important to Aquinas was the great Jewish scholar **Maimonides** (see entry), also a commentator on Aristotle. Both Averroës and Maimonides had lived in the previous century, and both had tried to explain Aristotle's philosophy in a way that was consistent with their religious beliefs. Their works were now circulating in Western cities like Naples. Averroës especially had a deep influence on Aquinas, who referred to Averroës simply as "the Commentator."

Dominicans. In Naples Aquinas also encountered members of a new order of monks, the Dominicans, founded in 1216 by St. Dominic. The Dominicans were becoming known for their love of learning and for their pursuit of academic studies within the framework of the monk's life. When Aquinas informed his mother that he had decided to join the Dominicans, not the more traditional Benedictines, she told his older brothers. Aquinas's father had

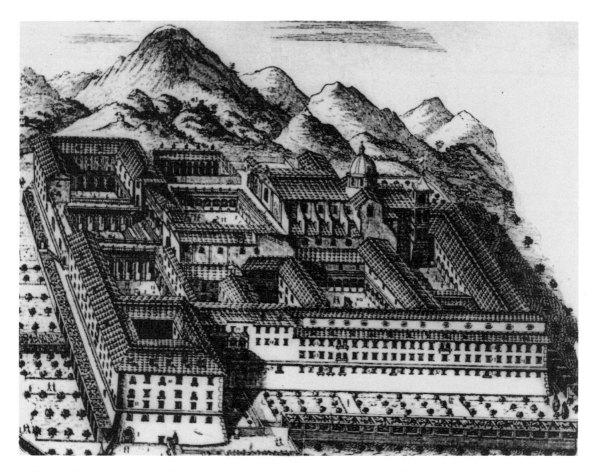

▲ Monte Cassino, where Thomas Aquinas was raised and educated.

recently died, so his brothers were in charge of the family. They ordered him back to the Benedictines. Aquinas refused. Probably to get him away from his family, the Dominicans sent him north, to Paris, but they were not fast enough. His family had him kidnapped from the monks with whom he was traveling. For a year they held him at home, but Aquinas never gave up. Seeing his determination to join the Dominicans, his family finally let him go.

Paris, Cologne, and Albert the Great. Aquinas was about twenty when he was accepted as a Dominican "novice," or new monk, in Naples. The order again sent him to Paris, to study at the new university there. This time, he made it safely. His activities in Paris are not well known, but among the subjects he certainly studied was theology, the study of God's nature and His relationship with humanity. Theology was considered the most important subject for medieval scholars. Aquinas continued to study Aristotle, for his teacher, Albert the Great (Albertus Magnus), a Dominican and a man of many interests, was caught up, like so many others, in Aristotle's newly rediscovered works. In fact, he made them his specialty. In 1248 Albert was assigned to start a new university in his native Germany, at Cologne. Aquinas went to Cologne, too, where he continued his studies with Albert for four more years.

Albert was one of the first Westerners to understand how important it was for Christian theology to do what Averroës and Maimonides had done—to accept the challenge of ancient philosophy. Like Averroës and Maimonides, he wrote many commentaries on Aristotle. Aquinas, his most famous pupil, would follow in his footsteps. Though he would disagree with Albert on some points, Aquinas's work built on Albert's, especially in putting forth human reason as an important part of Christian faith.

Teaching in Paris. In 1252 Aquinas progressed from student to teacher, returning to teach at the University of Paris for the next seven years. Along with teaching, Aquinas began the writings that would eventually make him famous. The titles of these early works reflect a mix of theology and philosophy based on Aristotle's groundbreaking ideas. *On Being and Essence, On the Principles of Nature, On the Holy Trinity, Disputed Questions on Truth,* and a commentary on the Gospel of Matthew are among the works Aquinas wrote in these years. At the same time, he produced essays defending the Dominicans against critics. The new scholarly orders, the Dominicans and Franciscans (established by St. Francis in 1209), upset those who preferred to cling to old ways. One such writer claimed that the monks' activities surely meant that the end of the world was just around the corner.

After several years as an apprentice teacher, Aquinas received his *licentia docendi,* "teaching license," in 1256, along with the degree of master of theology.

Italy. Aquinas left Paris and returned to his native Italy, where he served as a sort of traveling teacher. In this era of new ideas, the Church needed to keep up with the latest develop-ments. So from 1259 to 1268, Aquinas traveled to Dominican monasteries in towns all over central and northern Italy, teach-ing theology to his brother monks. According to the Domini-cans' rules, he was not allowed to ride a horse or donkey, or use any kind of vehicle. All his traveling had to be by foot, so Aquinas spent long days between assignments trudging Italy's dusty mountain trails and winding coastal roads. He began with two years at the Dominican monastery in Anagni, near Rome. In 1261 he began four years in the hilltop town of Orvieto, where Pope Urban VI had set up his headquarters. He returned to Rome in 1265 to spend two years at the monastery of Santa Sabina. Aquinas spent shorter periods between these assignments in other towns.

William of Moerbeke. It was in Orvieto (where his old teacher Albert the Great was then also stationed) that Aquinas met William of Moerbeke, a Dominican from what is today Belgium. William was one of the few scholars in the West who had learned ancient Greek,

Challenge to Faith

Christianity, like Islam and Judaism, had always stressed faith—that is, accepting religious beliefs without calling for any kind of proof. Aristotle's ideas emphasized the power of people to understand things rationally—that is, with their ability to rea-son or think logically—and to weigh such factors as evidence and proof. Aristotle thus seemed to challenge the very idea of faith.

Aristotle's language. At Aquinas's request, the story goes, William now began to make new and more accurate translations of Aristo-tle so that scholars would no longer have to rely on Arabic ver-sions of the Greek philosopher's writings. William's translations became famous, adding to the wave of enthusiasm for Aristotle that was sweeping Europe's young universities.

Averroists. In late 1268 or early 1269, Aquinas was assigned to teach again at the University of Paris. Once more he made the long walk north. This time he stayed for three years, continuing his writing and teaching. He also became more deeply involved in conflicts that had arisen over how Aristotle's ideas should be applied to theology. Some scholars had taken up Averroës' posi-tion, claiming that faith and reason were totally separate and one was not based upon the other. Thus, Aristotle's ideas about man's rational nature did not threaten Christian faith, they said. For these so-called "Latin Averroists", Aristotle and Averroës stood for reason in its purest form. Therefore, they rejected any attempt to make room for faith in Aristotle's philosophy.

Though influenced by Averroës, Aquinas believed that faith and reason could fit together, rather than side-by-side, as the Averroists claimed. All truths come from God, he argued, which makes them in a sense one single truth. According to Aquinas then, faith and reason are just different ways of explaining that truth.

Augustinians. Opposing the Averroists were the Augustinians, who adhered to the ideas of St. Augustine. This great African theologian and philosopher (354-430) was the most important influence on Christian theology before Aquinas. His teachings, emphasizing faith, had become the traditional position of most Christian thinkers. St. Augustine's followers now led the way in rejecting Aristotle and the new ideas that had arisen from his works. Aquinas's findings fell between these two enemy camps and he was thus often attacked by both. Students and teachers alike took sides. Sometimes classes had to be canceled, for students protested then just as they do now, and these were the issues they felt strongly about. Aquinas's views would not win widespread acceptance until after his death.

Death on the road from Naples. In 1272 Aquinas headed back to Italy. He had been assigned to establish a Dominican house at the University of Naples, the learning center of his youth. He kept up his teaching and writing there, finishing the major theological works he had started years before as well as his commentaries on Aristotle. In early 1274 he prepared to retrace his steps north once again in order to attend an important meeting of church leaders in Lyons, France. The pope had summoned Aquinas per-

Miracles

Aquinas's brilliant writing was not the only factor led the Catholic Church to declare him a saint. Stories were told of miracles associated with him (miracles are necessary for the Church to declare someone a saint). Once, while writing, Aquinas became puzzled about the meaning of a certain part of the Bible. He fasted and prayed, but he still couldn't make sense of it. Then, his friend Reginald of Piperno, walking by Aquinas's room, heard him talking to someone inside. Aquinas was able to finish his writing. Later, after repeated questioning by Reginald, Aquinas finally admitted that he had been visited by St. Peter and St. Paul, who had helped him with the problem. Both saints, of course, had been dead for many centuries. Another time, Aquinas was observed praying in church—hovering several feet off the floor.

sonally. Aquinas was most likely ill before leaving Naples, and when he stopped off to visit his niece in Maenza, he became too sick to continue. A few days later, he was moved to a nearby monastery at Fossanova. There, on March 7, 1274, Aquinas died. He was forty-nine.

Aftermath

Philosopher, theologian, saint. During the fourteenth century, as the dust settled from the great religious debates of the thirteenth century, Aquinas's reputation in the Church grew and grew. The Catholic Church ultimately adopted many of his views as its own, and in 1323 he was declared a saint. His beliefs, called "Thomism," continue to be highly influential in both theology and philosophy.

Major Works

Though Aquinas left an impressive number of works, his most famous are two summaries of Catholic doctrine (official beliefs): *Summa contra gentiles* ("Summary against the Non-Christians," 1264), and *Summa Theologica* ("Summary of Theology," 1273).

For More Information

Gilson, Etienne. *History of Christian Philosophy in the Middle Ages.* New York: Random House, 1955.

McInerny, Ralph. *St. Thomas Aquinas.* Boston: Twayne, 1977.

Pegis, Anton, editor. *Introduction to Saint Thomas Aquinas.* New York: Modern Library, 1948.

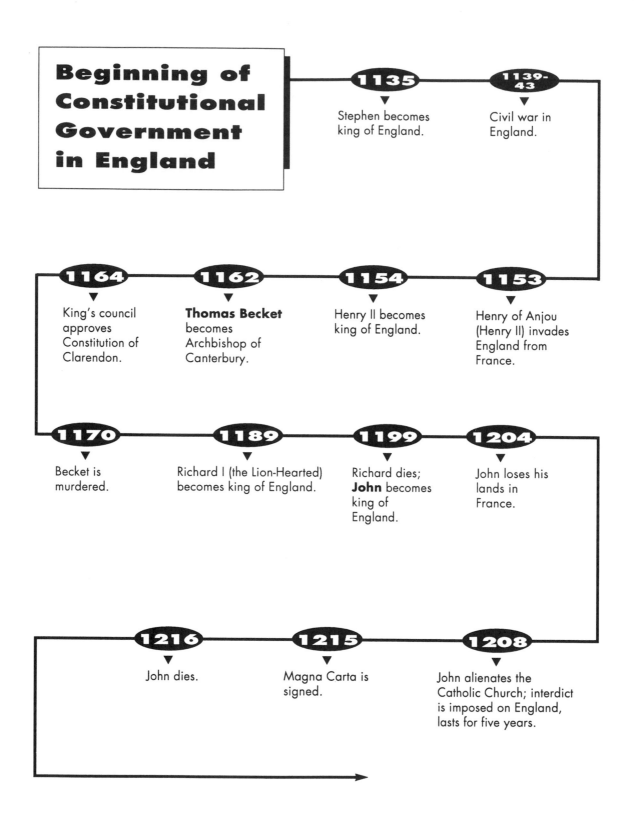

Beginning of Constitutional Government in England

1135
▼
Stephen becomes king of England.

1139-43
▼
Civil war in England.

1164
▼
King's council approves Constitution of Clarendon.

1162
▼
Thomas Becket becomes Archbishop of Canterbury.

1154
▼
Henry II becomes king of England.

1153
▼
Henry of Anjou (Henry II) invades England from France.

1170
▼
Becket is murdered.

1189
▼
Richard I (the Lion-Hearted) becomes king of England.

1199
▼
Richard dies; **John** becomes king of England.

1204
▼
John loses his lands in France.

1216
▼
John dies.

1215
▼
Magna Carta is signed.

1208
▼
John alienates the Catholic Church; interdict is imposed on England, lasts for five years.

BEGINNING OF CONSTITUTIONAL GOVERNMENT IN ENGLAND

William the Conqueror, the Duke of Normandy, a region in northern France, took control of England in a one-day war in 1066. He established a strong central government with sectional governors. They presided over small fiefdoms managed by powerful enforcers, the sheriffs. In addition, he ordered the most complete census of England up to that time in order to levy and collect taxes from everyone.

Stephen. None of William's successors, however, could match his strong and effective rule. William was followed by Henry I, his fourth son, who had taken advantage of his eldest brother's participation in the First Crusade to take over the throne. He controlled the land with great diplomatic skill but was almost constantly interrupted by challenges to his rule. Henry I was succeeded by his nephew and William's grandson, Stephen, raised to the office over his mother through intrigue. He almost immediately separated himself from his brother, the Bishop of Winchester, and the lords (wealthy landowners, also called barons) who had supported his selection. Lacking the backing of either the Church or the landowners and threatened by the possible return to England of his mother, Matilda, Stephen's rule was particularly weak. Once again, power fell into the hands of ambitious lords, and the countryside decayed into lawlessness.

Henry II. Such was the situation when Henry II took the throne in 1154. Although given to fits of uncontrollable anger, Henry proved to be an able ruler. He brought the landowners once again under royal rule and began to strengthen the justice system. Over time, he was able to gather strong support from the lords of the land, from which he formed a council to advise him in government. Thus involved, the lords helped reestablish a strong central government. There remained a single, formidable obstacle to the establishment of a sovereign government in England—the Catholic Church.

Church versus state. Even William the Conqueror had hesitated to challenge Church authority and its intervention in English politics and government. Particularly offensive to Henry was Church involvement in the courts. While he formed a national court system and appointed supervisors who continuously monitored the workings of the justice system, the Catholic Church insisted on maintaining its own courts. The Church insisted that it had the right to try its own clergy, of which there were many, for crimes committed either against the Church or against people who were not Church officials. Thus, a clergyman might rob one of the parishioners, be tried by a Church court, and receive little or no penalty. Henry II estimated that in the first few years of his rule, more than a hundred murderers had been released or received only light sentences because of this "benefit of clergy." He wanted to bring the wayward clergy to accountability in the civil courts.

This issue came to a head when a clergyman killed a commoner and was let off with only a light fine by the Church court. In the resulting uproar, Henry demanded that the clergyman be released to the civil court. He was opposed by the leader of the Catholic Church in England, the Archbishop of Canterbury, **Thomas Becket,** who had been Henry's good friend and England's prime minister. The struggle between the two grew into a deep rift as Henry tried to redesign the court system. Becket's murder by knights loyal to Henry (though acting alone) postponed the issue and prolonged the power struggle between church and state for decades.

King John. Richard I, the Lion-Hearted succeeded his father, Henry II, but was much more interested in the family holdings that made up almost half of France than he was in England. Richard was also preoccupied with the Third Crusade; he spent only ten months of his ten-year reign in England. His successor, **King John,** was so ruthless and greedy that he turned his subjects and world leaders against him. He lost the king's lands in France and subsequently concentrated on England.

But John's concern about England was linked to his need for taxation to support his lavish lifestyle. Collecting money from lords and commoners alike to satisfy his tastes resulted in such antagonism toward him that the lords banded together to demand fairer treatment. They prepared a document defining the rights of the English aristocracy and demanded that the king sign it. The Magna Carta, as the document was called, paid little attention to the English commoners. In addition, it wasn't initially very effective; John used his armed forces to subdue the lords and maintained his despotic rule until his death, though the lords continued to resist.

Nevertheless, the Magna Carta was an early declaration of citizens' rights and is hailed as the beginning of English constitutional rule. Thus the actions taken against Becket and John were steps toward forming a representative government that would eventually rule over a worldwide British Empire.

Thomas Becket

c. 1118-1170

Personal Background

Early life. Thomas Becket was born in London, December 21, circa 1118. His father, Gilbert, was a prosperous merchant. Both father and mother had migrated to London from France—Gilbert from Rouen, and Becket's mother from Caen. History did not record his mother's name, though there is some speculation that she was of Middle Eastern ancestry. At any rate, Becket was raised in a privileged home. Handsome and bright, he received the best possible education, first in a church school in Surrey, then studying at Oxford, London, and Paris. He was preparing for a career in the Church.

Becket returned from studies in Paris at age twenty-two to find that his parents had fallen on hard times. He was forced to abandon his plans for a career in the Church and become a clerk in the business of a relative. This turned out to be fortunate, for the relative was well connected in London politics. Through him, Becket was introduced to Theobald, the Archbishop of Canterbury and the most powerful Church authority in all of England. Becket was taken into Theobald's family.

Aide to the archbishop. Becket accompanied Theobald to Church meetings in Rome and in Reims, France. He also studied Church and lay law in Germany and France. By the time he was thirty-four, he had become so well trained that Theobald sent him

▲ **Thomas Becket**

Event: Defining the roles of church and state in England.

Role: As Archbishop of Canterbury, head of the Catholic Church in England, Thomas Becket stubbornly resisted the efforts of King Henry II to include members of the Church clergy in his reformation of the English court system. His actions prolonged the friction between England's church and lay courts throughout the Middle Ages.

on a special mission to Rome. He was to plead with the pope not to approve the coronation of the son of Stephen, the feeble king who had allowed England to revert to a fragmented, lawless land governed by numerous powerful nobles. His success in this mission made it possible for Henry II to take the English throne in 1154.

Chancellor of England. Henry II was so impressed that in 1155 he appointed Becket chancellor in his government, a position similar to that of prime minister. Becket enjoyed this position and its wealth. He entertained lavishly, and it was said that he never passed a day without giving a gift to someone of noble birth. He protected himself and those around him with a standing guard of seven hundred fully armed horsemen. The horses of this guard wore harnesses decorated in silver and gold.

Becket became Henry's friend and closest advisor as the king struggled to restore the power of the throne which had declined during the reign of Stephen. Henry had taken the throne when he was just twenty-one, and he valued the advice of the well-educated Becket, who was perhaps thirteen years older.

Friend of the king. Becket made the most of his friendship with the king. When it became necessary for the king to protect his land in Toulouse, France (Henry owned more French land than the king of France), Becket supported him by sending seven hundred soldiers with twelve hundred horses. The king was impressed, even more so when Becket was able to arrange Henry's marriage to the daughter of the king of France.

Restoring a strong government. Henry believed it was his duty to restore a strong government to England. William the Conqueror had begun this task by breaking up the kingdoms of the powerful lords, establishing a court system, and bringing his own Norman people in as landowners. Henry I continued to strengthen the power of the king, but his successor, Stephen, had allowed the large landowners (lords) to again become strong and

▶

Detail from the Thomas Becket window at Canterbury Cathedral;
as both prime minister and head of the English church,
Becket would bring the church more in line with the
court policies King Henry II wanted—or so the king thought.

to take the law into their own hands. Henry II began by again reorganizing the landholdings and by establishing a system of national courts. His agents regularly traveled the country overseeing the actions of these courts. Gradually, he took over the legal powers of the lords.

There was, however, one court system that was a constant obstacle to the total rule of the king—the Church courts. Even William the Conqueror had been unwilling to challenge these courts, and the Church had continued to insist that its own courts try people associated with the Church. In Thomas Becket Henry had a friend and ally who he felt could help him with this problem of controlling the Church.

Chancellor and archbishop. When Theobald died, Henry saw an opportunity to strengthen his position. There was at that time a very weak pope, Alexander III, who had been forced to flee Rome and establish his rule in France. It was easy, therefore, for Henry to name Becket the new Archbishop of Canterbury in 1162 and to have this confirmed by the pope—though Becket was not even a priest. As both chancellor and head of the Church in England, Becket would certainly bring the Church more in line with the court policies Henry supported—so the king thought.

Participation: Defining the Roles of Church and State in England

An about-face. No sooner had Becket been confirmed as archbishop than he made a complete change in his life. He abandoned his fine clothes and rich lifestyle. Instead, he announced his change from a secular life to a religious life by wearing sackcloth and by entertaining the poor and homeless rather than the nobles.

One of his first acts as archbishop was to attend a conference called by the pope, where he spoke against replacing Church law with kingly law. Becket soon discovered that he could not be both chancellor and archbishop. He could not be totally loyal to the king and also to the pope. Becket chose loyalty to the pope.

The "Constitution of Clarendon." Henry was outraged by Becket's new loyalty to the Church. He was further incensed when a Church worker killed a man and was tried in a Church court. When that court gave the guilty man a very light sentence, Henry asked Becket to allow such cases to be tried in government courts. Becket refused, and the rift between him and the king widened. Henry was, however, a resourceful and powerful king and had already begun to bring the country's nobles and bishops around to his way of thinking. In 1164 he gathered them at Clarendon to approve the Constitution of Clarendon, which contained his changes to English law. The changes cut deeply into the authority of the Church. If a bishopric or abbey became temporarily without a leader, for example, the new laws gave the king the right to manage the Church property. All legal disputes involving clergymen were to be tried in government courts. Judges could decide to try a clergyman in civil court and have punishment prescribed by that court. No officer of the court could be excommunicated from the Church without the king's approval. No son of a peasant could be ordained into the ministry without the consent of the lord he served. All legal appeals were to be heard by the king, not the pope. High-ranking members of the clergy could not leave England without the king's consent.

If all these rules had been put into effect, the Church would have given up most of its power. But the new laws had to have the approval of the Archbishop of Canterbury, and Becket refused to sign them. His old friends among the nobles and bishops pleaded with him. For a time, he seemed about to sign, but then refused again. Henry was angry. Becket was arrested for misusing funds as chancellor, tried, found guilty, and fined. Twice more he was arrested and fined. Finally, he realized that the king would not rest until he had changed his views. The archbishop was forced to flee England for France. For a while, he lived in an abbey at Pontigny in Normandy. When the king brought pressure to have him removed, he escaped to another abbey, where he stayed for four years. While there, the archbishop prepared letters of excommunication for the bishops who had voted against the Church, the Archbishop of York, who had performed some duties for the king without the approval of the Archbishop of Canterbury (see box), and even the king himself.

Resignation, reinstatement, and reconciliation. For six years, Becket remained in exile. He offered his resignation to the pope and was immediately reappointed Archbishop of Canterbury. During this time, Henry worried about his own relationship with the pope. Few kings of that day could afford to make enemies with the head of the Church. Then, too, the archbishop remained very popular in England. The peasants saw him as a champion of their causes, an ally in their campaign to lighten the heavy hand of the king. At last, Henry engineered a truce with Becket, and the archbishop returned to England in 1170.

Return of the archbishop. The people of England were very happy. Becket was met by a welcoming crowd so large that it must have given the king second thoughts. But any idea he may have had about a change in archbishop was soon dispelled as Becket began to deliver his excommunications.

Henry demanded that the archbishop recall the excommunications, and Becket refused. The king was infuriated. He stormed around the castle roaring that his followers were a pack of cowards. He complained that not one of them would step forward to put an end to the torment he suffered because of Becket. Four of his knights heard his rantings and decided that it was a call for someone to kill the archbishop. They conspired to do it.

> ## Confrontation Between King and Archbishop
>
> The quarrel between Henry II and Thomas Becket came to a head over Henry's wish to crown his eldest son as viceroy of England. Becket and the pope contended that only the Archbishop of Canterbury could crown the new viceroy. But since Becket was in exile over his dispute with the king, the Archbishop of York was persuaded to crown the viceroy. For this act, Becket excommunicated (removed from the church) the Archbishop of York and the bishops who supported him and the king.

Death of Becket. The archbishop was in the cathedral at prayer when the four men arrived. With swords drawn they went in to where Becket was praying and tried to drag him from the church. When he resisted, they killed him where he prayed.

The uproar caused by the murder accomplished Becket's aim—the new laws Henry had proposed were never enacted.

► **The murder of Thomas Becket; the uproar over Becket's death accomplished what he couldn't do in life: the new laws Henry proposed were never enacted.**

This was the only major setback for the king, however, who continued to rule until his own wife and sons united to replace him. One son, Henry, was actually crowned King of England while Henry II was still alive.

Aftermath

Sainthood. Becket was canonized (declared a saint) in 1173. The four murderers were forced to confess and ask forgiveness. All four made a pilgrimage to Jerusalem to show their regret. Henry, though he had little if anything to do with the murder, showed his remorse by kneeling on Becket's blood in the cathedral as he prayed for forgiveness. He later did penance before the image of the new saint—Saint Thomas.

Murderers of Thomas Becket

Four knights close to King Henry II took it upon themselves to kill the archbishop. They were led by Reginald FitzUrse. With him were William de Tracy, Hugh de Morville, and Richard Brito. All struck Becket in Canterbury Cathedral until "the blood white with the brain, and the brain red with blood, dyed the surface of the virgin mother church " (Cheney, p. 158).

Church and state. The king's immediate successors paid little attention to the division of power between church and state. Richard the Lion-Hearted spent his reign in France and on the Third Crusade to recover Jerusalem, and **John** (see entry) was a tyrant who spent much of his time devising new ways to squeeze tax dollars out of his subjects. But from time to time, the issue of who would control the judicial system of England resurfaced, and other differences between church and state arose. Almost four centuries after Becket's death, in 1534, Henry VIII settled the matter by separating England from the Catholic Church altogether, creating the Church of England.

For More Information

Cheney, E. P. *Readings in English History Drawn from the Original Sources.* Boston: Ginn, 1908.

Knowles, D. The Monastic Order in England 940-1216. Cambridge, England: Cambridge University Press, 1963.

McElwee, William. *A Short History of England.* New York: Frederick A. Praeger, 1969.

Morgan, Kenneth O., editor. The Oxford Illustrated History of Britain. Oxford, England: Oxford University Press, 1984.

King John

1167-1216

Personal Background

Christmas child. John was born on Christmas Eve in 1167 at Oxford, England. He was the fourth son of one of England's greatest kings, Henry II. John's mother was Eleanor of Aquitaine, which was a province of southern France. Henry had already inherited Normandy and other parts of France from his ancestor William the Conqueror. Gaining Aquitaine through marriage had given him fiefdoms in France that amounted to more land than was controlled by the king of that country. Thus John was born into a royal and wealthy family, in which he rapidly became the favorite of his father. But John was a prince without land. In fact, he was known as Prince John Lackland. Henry had divided his great holdings between his older sons—one of whom, Richard (also known as Richard the Lion-hearted), would eventually rule over England and Normandy.

King Henry's favorite. When John was still young, Henry tried to develop a land base for his son. At the age of five, John was betrothed (promised) in marriage to the heiress of Maurienne and Savoy in southern France. That would have given John ownership of an important land route between France and Italy. But this betrothal never resulted in a wedding. Instead, when he was older but still a boy, it became politically important for Henry to seal his own power with the Earl of Gloucester, a powerful ruler

▲ **King John**

Event: Signing the Magna Carta.

Role: The greedy and arrogant King John so mismanaged and mistreated his subjects that an assemblage of nobles prepared a document defining their own rights and forced the king to sign it. Although not immediately effective and failing to encompass the mass of English people, this document, the Magna Carta, directed the English government toward a parliamentary system.

of part of England. John was again betrothed—to Isabella, the earl's daughter. Meanwhile, Henry tried to establish his favorite son by giving him part of the land promised to his older brother, Richard. Richard would not tolerate this however, and a rift separated the king and his eldest son. This rift would later erupt into a rebellion.

Ruler of Ireland. When John was twenty, Henry made one more effort to establish his son as a ruler. John was made Lord of Ireland. It took John only a few years to make enemies of the Irish nobles through his program of taxation and his insolence toward them. John was forced to abandon his rule in Ireland and return to London.

First conspiracy. Despite his arrogance, John remained his father's favorite. By 1186 two of John's older brothers had died. Concerned that his father would turn on him, Richard appealed to Phillip of France, and the two joined to overthrow Henry. When John joined them in the revolt, Henry was emotionally defeated. He died in 1189, leaving England and Normandy to Richard. Brittany, a large section of northwestern France, was awarded to Henry's grandson, Arthur.

Family of King John

John married twice. His first wife was Isabella of Gloucester, whose marriage to him was arranged by his father, Henry II. His second wife was Isabella of Angouléne. With her John had two sons, Henry III and Richard, and three daughters: Joan, who married the king of Scotland; Isabella who married Frederick II; and Eleanor, whose husband Simon de Montfort governed England after Henry III. John also fathered four illegitimate sons and one daughter.

Richard the Lion-Hearted. Richard lived in Normandy and spent little time in England before or after he took the throne. He had not been on the throne long when news came from the East of the terrible treatment Christians were receiving at the hands of a Muslim ruler. Richard joined the Third Crusade to take Christian control of Jerusalem and other parts of the Middle East. It was 1189. He had already decided that his nephew Arthur would be his heir, but before he left for the Holy Land Richard changed his mind and made John the heir to England and Normandy.

It was possible for Richard to go off to crusade because of the efficient organization his father had built. Henry had divided

England and Normandy into sections, like counties or states, and had given responsibility for taxing and judging to local governments. These were thus well governed even when the king was away. Richard simply left the overall management of the kingdom to his prime minister, who was also Archbishop of Canterbury. No one knew that Richard would be gone for several years.

Second conspiracy. Richard was two years into his crusade when he heard that his old friend Phillip and his brother were conspiring to overthrow him. Richard immediately headed home, but on the way he was taken prisoner in Austria. John took advantage of his brother's imprisonment to take further steps toward seizing the English throne. Some reports say that the conniving and unscrupulous young brother actually sent letters to the ruler in Austria asking that Richard not be released.

By this time, Richard had not been in England for more than five years, but he was still very popular there. When the Austrian government demanded a huge ransom for his release, the lords of England gladly taxed themselves to pay it. By 1194 one-third of the ransom had been collected and Richard was released. (The English would tax themselves again and again to pay the rest of the ransom.) Richard, perhaps feeling that he could watch his double-crossing brother more easily if they made peace, forgave John for trying to take over his throne.

King John. Richard died in 1199, leaving John the throne of England and Normandy. Nephew Arthur, only twelve years old, controlled Brittany, and John's mother, Eleanor, governed Aquitaine. Now the undisputed ruler, John proceeded to mistreat nearly everyone. He taxed the English people until many of them were starving. He insulted the barons (wealthy landowners), bishops, and priests alike.

As his reign wore on, John continued to tax unjustly and to spend money on questionable projects. The barons continued to oppose him. Some of them would have preferred to have Arthur on the throne. But in 1203 Arthur was murdered on the Seine River. At the time, John was visiting France. Some say he arranged the murder; others say John killed Arthur himself.

The uproar over Arthur's death gave King Phillip of France his opportunity. He declared that by this act John had forfeited his claim to Normandy and other parts of France. John's efforts to gather an army to defend Normandy proved very expensive to the English taxpayers, who had already taxed themselves heavily to pay off Richard's ransom. Even so, John could not gather a fighting force strong enough to regain Normandy. By 1204 the king of England had lost his holdings in France and was forced to remain in England.

Heavy taxes and injustice. John now spent his time thinking of ways to regain his lost land, taxing the people to pay for his follies. A few barons supported his travel throughout England, Scotland, and Ireland—everywhere making sure that his demands were met and everywhere mistreating his subjects, imprisoning them and ordering them tortured with little or no cause. John's financial antics resulted in high inflation in England and, while the people starved, he levied even more taxes and placed tight controls over the rich English forest lands.

> ### Murder of Arthur
>
> "They took the prince from his dungeon and rowed out in a small boat on the Seine. Arthur was in great fear and begged his uncle to spare his life, promising to do whatever he wished if he would only allow him to live. But the wretch made a signal to De Maulac, who refused to do the horrible deed, whereupon the King himself drove a dagger into the body of the poor youth and flung his body overboard. There is little room for doubt that Arthur was slain in this dreadful manner, for no more was ever heard of him" (Ellis and Horne, p. 1003).

John and the Pope. It is perhaps no surprise that John quarreled with the Roman Catholic Church. He and Pope Innocent III disagreed on the appointment of a new Archbishop of Canterbury in 1206 and were for many years enemies. Then, two years later, John found he needed more money and plundered the English churches to rob the clergy. Innocent III was furious and placed an "interdict" on all of England. That meant that the bishops and priests could not hold church services or conduct such religious rites as weddings and funerals. For six years, no church bells rang in England. That did not bother John, though, and in

◄
John submits to King Richard the Lion-Hearted; Richard forgave his brother for trying to take over his throne.

1209 the pope took stronger action—he excommunicated John from the Church. John responded by seizing the property of the Church in England.

By 1212 the barons of England had decided that they could no longer abide the king's practices. Some of them asked Phillip to invade England and take charge. John heard of the plot and quickly put it down, but he began feeling alienated. Only a few barons supported him, and he had made an enemy of the Church. In 1213 the English king took an unusual step to shore up his failing support—he asked to be reinstated in the Church; in return, he would give all of England to the pope. John would continue to rule as head of a papal fiefdom. That was acceptable to the pope, who could now demand thousands of dollars in taxes each year.

Rebellious barons. By 1214 those taxes had grown to nearly one-third of England's income. In addition, John had decided to take one more military excursion to try to win back his French lands. When this task failed, the barons decided that they must again take action to end John's ruinous reign. If there had been a reasonable replacement, they might have forced John's ouster and installed a new king. But Arthur was gone, John's sons were too young, and other candidates were unpopular foreigners. The barons decided on governmental reform instead of replacing the king.

Participation: Signing the Magna Carta

The baronial demands. The most powerful barons had been planning to act for more than a year. They had met in council and had begun to prepare rules of government intended to protect the rich landowners' rights. By 1215 they had written out sixty-three articles stating their positions on a piece of parchment.

The barons prepared further by taking control of London. Then they arranged a meeting with John on June 15, 1215, at a meadow called Runnymede, on the banks of the Thames River. There John was shown the document and given no choice but to sign it. The angry king signed the most famous document in English history—the Magna Carta.

▲ King John signing the Magna Carta; John was determined that the articles of the Magna Carta would not be enforced, and during his lifetime he made every effort to see that nothing came of it.

Magna Carta. The Magna Carta covered a wide range of issues, touching not only on the separation of the state from the Church, but providing for uniform weights and measures and requiring that river transportation be improved by removing dams and weirs (fences to catch fish). Over the years the document underwent many changes, but a few of the articles remained to establish the form of government of the British Empire. For example:

- No free man was to be imprisoned or proceeded against except by his peers or equals, or by the accepted laws of the land.

- Justice was not to be sold, denied, or delayed.

- A national council (later "Great Council") of barons was to be formed with the right to remove a king.

- No taxes were to be imposed without the approval of the council of barons.

- The government was not to impose levies or fines on the barons that would endanger their livelihood.

- The Church would be allowed to hold free elections, without the approval of the king.

Other statutes were more immediate. The sheriffs who had been installed by kings since Henry II to enforce local laws had grown oppressive. One article, therefore, restricted the power of the sheriffs.

The end of John. John left the meeting incensed. He was determined that the articles of the Magna Carta would not be enforced, and during his lifetime he made every effort to see that nothing came of the document. He called for help from the pope, who saw that the Church's tax base would be eroded by the Magna Carta and declared it invalid. John became more and more unpopular as he rode with his band of supporters around England, taxing, fining, and imprisoning his subjects. He was so hated that it became necessary for him to sleep in a different house each night to avoid becoming the victim of foul play. And it became his custom to cover his tracks by burning the house he slept in as he left it. Within a year of signing the Magna Carta, the man who would go down in history as one of England's most inefficient rulers died—some say from frustration, some claim from overeating (peaches and ale), and some claim by poison. He died "a knight without truth, a king without justice, and a Christian without faith" (Ellis and Horne, p. 1005).

Aftermath

New king. When John died, his son, Henry III, was named king, though some desperate barons had offered the crown to Louis, son of the king of France. Louis even brought an army to England. But he rewarded his followers with so much English land that the barons decided on the nine-year-old Henry to lead them instead. Good counselors and administrators were provided to help him and, for a time, the country was run smoothly. But the adult Henry proved to be as unscrupulous as his father and an even worse administrator. He was eventually replaced in a rebellion led by his brother-in-law Simon de Montfort. Known as Righteous Simon, this ruler of England opened the Magna Carta to a broader range of the citizenry. He believed that the Great Council should represent more than just the barons and decided that two representatives of each town and borough would also serve on the council. The Great Council began to call itself Parliament. The Magna Carta had led to the beginnings of the present form of government in Britain.

For More Information

Ellis, Edward S., and Charles F. Horne. *The World's Famous Events.* New York: Francis R. Niglutsch, 1913.

McElwee, William. *A Short History of England.* New York: Frederick A. Praeger, 1968.

Morgan, Kenneth O. *Oxford Illustrated History of Britain.* Oxford, England: Oxford University Press, 1984.

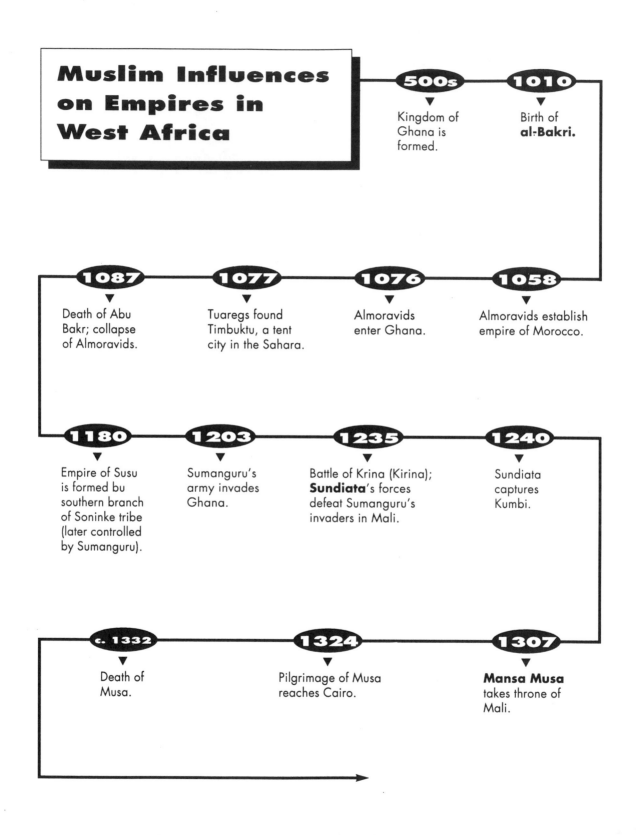

Muslim Influences on Empires in West Africa

500s — Kingdom of Ghana is formed.

1010 — Birth of **al-Bakri.**

1058 — Almoravids establish empire of Morocco.

1076 — Almoravids enter Ghana.

1077 — Tuaregs found Timbuktu, a tent city in the Sahara.

1087 — Death of Abu Bakr; collapse of Almoravids.

1180 — Empire of Susu is formed bu southern branch of Soninke tribe (later controlled by Sumanguru).

1203 — Sumanguru's army invades Ghana.

1235 — Battle of Krina (Kirina); **Sundiata**'s forces defeat Sumanguru's invaders in Mali.

1240 — Sundiata captures Kumbi.

1307 — **Mansa Musa** takes throne of Mali.

1324 — Pilgrimage of Musa reaches Cairo.

c. 1332 — Death of Musa.

MUSLIM INFLUENCES ON EMPIRES IN WEST AFRICA

Instructed to explore the world by the prophet Muhammad, Arab peoples spread across northern Africa in the seventh and eighth centuries A.D. They joined with Berber tribesmen to form the Almoravids, who established the kingdom of Morocco, occupied southern Spain, and explored the Sahara Desert. Eventually, the Almoravids worked their way from Morocco to the Sudan, the great grassland south of the Sahara Desert between the Atlantic Ocean and Nile River.

Ghana. These were not the first people from northern Africa to penetrate the south. As early as the fourth century, northerners had moved into the Sudan to find small bands of hunters and farmers living on the Niger River. The North Africans introduced a new political order to the region, which resulted, by the ninth century, in a powerful kingdom that ruled the area north of the Niger and Senegal rivers. At first this kingdom, Ghana, was ruled by North Africans, but by the ninth century the black southern Africans had regained control of the area. Word of the kingdom of Ghana spread to Europe in various ways: early North African visitors to the Sudan brought back stories of the people and wealth of the south; and Ghana quickly established a reputation for trade, transporting gold and slaves to the edge of the desert to be taken north and east.

North and south were soon carrying on a vigorous trade across the Sahara Desert. Merchants brought goods from Europe and the Middle East to ports along the Mediterranean Sea. The products were loaded onto horses and donkeys and transported to the edge of the desert. The loads were again transferred at posts along the northern Sahara, where they were taken across the desert on camels. Towns sprung up along the southern edge of the desert and along the Niger River, serving as trading centers for the people of the Sudan.

Ghana, one of the first kingdoms to mix trade and agriculture, became a large and wealthy state. Its people, however, had no written language, so knowledge of their history was limited to the oral histories of their *griots*, or storytellers, and to the memories of traders who visited there. Today, the best information about the old kingdom of Ghana comes from men who assembled historical writings, combined them with reports from travelers of the time, and prepared new historical and geographical records. One of the earliest of these historians was an eleventh-century geographer named **al-Bakri.**

Muslim influence. Most of the traders across the desert from Ghana were Muslims. Many citizens of West Africa adopted Islam either out of religious conviction or to make trading easier. It became necessary for Ghana to build twin cities at its capital of Kumbi (now in part of Mali)—one city for the king of Ghana and his staff; another for Muslim traders, of which there were a growing number.

The extremely devout Almoravids, meanwhile, were advancing around the west coast of Africa. By the ninth century these Muslims were pressing on the borders of Ghana. The kings of Ghana were able to muster large numbers of soldiers, who, although not well armed, managed to fend off the invading Muslims for many years. Finally, though, the Almoravids, directed by a strongman named Abu Bakr, stormed the country, capturing Kumbi, killing many of the Ghanaians, and forcing others to accept Islam. Just as suddenly, the death of Abu Bakr a decade later brought a decline in the rule of the Muslims and a resurgence, if only for a short time, of the kingdom of Ghana.

After Ghana. After the decline of Ghana, another power just south of Ghana, Susu, arose under the tyrant ruler Sumanguru and for a moment threatened to overtake the region. Sumanguru, however, had made enemies among the Mendé-speaking groups in the Sudan and the Muslim conclaves there. Mendé people and Muslims united under **Sundiata,** an heir to the small kingdom of Mali. Sumanguru was defeated, and Mali became a force for the unification of Muslim people in the area, rising out of the ashes of Ghana. Eventually, Mali would include all the land along the Niger and Senegal rivers from the Atlantic Ocean to the eastern edge of present-day Nigeria. At its peak, Mali's king **Mansa Musa** was the most powerful man in Africa.

Growing empires. The influence of Islam continued to grow. Sundiata professed to be a Muslim but continued to claim special powers as a mystic and magician (as was traditional for West African leaders). His son Uli demonstrated a deeper faith and became the first black African ruler to make the pilgrimage to the holy city of Mecca. Mansa Musa also embraced Islam, making such an extravaganza of his pilgrimage that, on a side trip, his entourage nearly destroyed the economy of Egypt by flooding it with gold and devaluing its currency. Additionally, he persuaded Islamic scholars to come to West Africa. He turned Timbuktu, a tent-city camel stop on the middle Niger, into a stronghold of Islamic learning and one of the most impressive market centers in Africa.

Thus Islam developed in the Sudan. Ancient Ghana evolved into ever larger empires—Susu, Mali, and then Songhay (Songhai)—until the present configuration of states in the Sudan took shape.

Al-Bakri

c. 1010-1094

Personal Background

Early life. Little is known of the early life of Abu Ubayd Abdallah ibn Abd Al-Aziz ibn Muhammad al-Bakri, except that he was born somewhere in the caliphate of Cordoba in southern Spain. His birthplace was probably near Huelva, a province about fifty miles west-southwest of Seville. His father was a wealthy landowner in the caliphate, and al-Bakri probably was a devout, well-educated Muslim. History begins to record his activities when he was twenty-one.

Cordoba. In the eleventh century, the Almoravids, a group of Muslim reformers in North Africa, grew powerful enough to found the empire of Morocco. Asked to come to the aid of Muslims already in Spain, they crossed over from Africa and eventually took control of Moorish Spain. At first Spain was ruled as a province of the region controlled by the caliph of North Africa, but eventually the Moors grew strong enough to break away and form a Spanish caliphate with headquarters at Cordoba. This caliphate presided over the Moors for nearly three centuries, warding off one challenge after another, though it eventually eroded.

Al-Bakri's family. In 1031, when al-Bakri was twenty-one, the caliph of Cordoba was overthrown. Al-Bakri's family took advantage of the ensuing confusion to declare their independence from the caliphate. The land they claimed included the provinces of

▲ **A 1535 map of the world; although he never left his native land, al-Bakri wrote books on the ancient kingdom of Ghana in West Africa.**

Event: Describing ancient Ghana for the Islamic world.

Role: Although he never left his native land in southern Spain, al-Bakri studied in its great Muslim centers of learning and lived in a seaport where great commerce with Africa was carried on. A careful observer and recorder, al-Bakri wrote *The Book of Roads and Kingdoms,* which described trade routes in Africa and the ancient kingdom of Ghana in West Africa—the southern center of trade across the Sahara Desert.

▲ Detail of a sixteenth-century painting of the port of Seville;
al-Bakri spent much of his time in the Spanish city.

Huelva and Saltes. Al-Bakri's father declared himself ruler of this
region, but he was soon overthrown by a more powerful Muslim,
al-Mutadid, and al-Bakri began his travels around southern Spain.

The family wealth allowed him to travel to Cordoba to study
under the great scholars who had assembled there. Ibn Hayyan, a

respected historian, and al-Udhri, an equally respected geographer, were there, and al-Bakri attached himself to them. History, geography, and writing were to become important subjects in his life.

Almeria and the Almoravids. His studies with the great scholars earned al-Bakri a reputation for scholarship himself. He was taken into the court of al-Mu'tasim, who controlled the seaport of Almeria, then as now a province on the southeast tip of Spain. Al-Bakri later spent much of his time in Seville. But it was during his years at the court at Almeria that he gathered information that would make him one of the great geographers.

The port of Almeria was one of the finest natural harbors on the Mediterranean Sea. Consequently, it served as a Muslim pirate stronghold for attacks on Christian sailors and merchants. It also served as a port of entry for trade to and from North Africa. Almeria was therefore an important station for gathering information about Africa, for the Almoravids had not been content to limit their rule to Morocco and Spain. The militants had pushed south around the coast of Africa until they were pounding on the borders of the first great kingdom in western West Africa, Ghana.

The Muslims were well aware of the riches of this black African nation. Gold and slaves had flowed from its capital at Kumbi across the Sahara Desert to markets in the north and east for many years. Also, the kingdom of Ghana had grown so powerful that it often threatened Muslim settlements in the desert. Although he never left his native land, al-Bakri gathered information in Almeria and sorted out truth from myth to write a geography book that detailed locations in Africa, *The Book of Roads and Kingdoms* (1070).

Participation:
Describing Ancient Ghana for the Islamic World

The routes of the Almoravids. Al-Bakri described the trade routes that had established Ghana as a leading trading partner of the Muslim Arabs and Berbers. They followed along the Atlantic coast to Aoudaghasi, then hugged the coast before turning toward the Ghana capital at Kumbi, then turned northeast to Walata and Timbuktu, a village on the upper Niger River at the edge of the Sahara Desert. Timbuktu had become a camel stop for caravans willing to take the more difficult routes across the desert. Al-Bakri noted the distances between the African cities and towns with such accuracy that his descriptions of the cities and the people were accepted as equally true.

Kumbi. Kumbi, the capital city of Ghana, was, according to al-Bakri, really two cities. One was a community of stone buildings and homes. There Muslim traders carried on a brisk trade in gold and salt. Ghana was rich in gold but lacked salt which was in great demand in the hot and humid region. The Muslim city of Kumbi (which seems to have been at that time called Ghanata), was large enough and rich enough to support at least twelve mosques.

The other city comprising Kumbi was located some distance from the Muslim city. According to al-Bakri, it contained the Ghanaians' sacred place, which was apparently a shrub-filled area around which was built a walled city nearly a mile square. The city's name, in fact, means "the forest." Perhaps thirty thousand people lived within its walls, and among its most important buildings were the king's palace and a single mosque for the use of visiting traders. The royal palace in Kumbi consisted of a fort and several huts. The palace fort was windowed and its walls were decorated with sculpture and paintings.

> ## Muslim Kumbi
>
> According to al-Bakri, the Muslim settlement at Kumbi was home to salaried Koranic readers and men of learning, and around it were "wells of sweet water from which they drink and near which they grow vegetables." The king's settlement some miles away had "a palace and a number of dome-shaped dwellings, the whole surrounded by an enclosure like the defensive wall of a city" (Al-Bakri in Davidson 1968, p. 80).

Al-Bakri and the people of Ghana. Some of the traditions of the black people of Ghana were shocking to al-Bakri, and he studied them so carefully that he sometimes wrote as if he had actually been to Africa to see the people firsthand.

He was a devout Muslim, a believer in a religion that, in his day, was very much male-dominated. He could hardly believe, then, that a new king of Ghana was not the son of the king but rather a son of the king's sister. Then, too, kings and other Ghana men mixed freely with the women in the court.

Nonetheless, al-Bakri was most impressed with the wealth of the kingdom of Ghana:

> The king adorns himself, as do the women here, with necklaces and bracelets; on their heads they wear caps decorated with gold, sewn on material of fine cotton stuffing.
>
> When he holds court ... [the king] sits in a pavilion around which stand ten horses wearing gold trappings; behind him ten pages stand holding shields and swords decorated with gold; at his right are the sons of the chiefs of the country, splendidly dressed and with their hair sprinkled with gold. (Al-Bakri in Oliver and Fage, p.10)

The king of Ghana. Al-Bakri described the incredible power of the king, held mostly through his subjects' fear of his magical powers but also by the might of his personal guard of a thousand soldiers. The king was also the chief judge and tax collector. All gold nuggets found in the country belonged to him. This king allowed his subjects to keep the gold dust they collected from the rivers and streams, perhaps because it was more difficult to handle than the gold stones.

By tradition, no one in the kingdom except the royal family was allowed to wear sewn clothing, which gave the king's household great status. All other Ghana citizens wore a single piece of cloth wrapped or draped around their bodies. The king was the absolute regulator of trade. His agents collected tariffs from every trader who entered the land. Al-Bakri reports that payment of a certain weight of gold was demanded for "every donkey-load of salt that enters the country" and twice as much for "every donkey-load of salt that goes out." In fact, the king of Ghana was so powerful that he carried two titles: *ghana,* meaning "war chief," and *kaya maghan,* "master to gold."

How al-Bakri knew about Ghana. Because the Spanish scholar had studied with one of the greatest historians of his time, he was no doubt inspired to read as much of Muslim geography and history as possible. Since Muslims had been traveling in Africa since the eighth century, some of what he wrote had already been recorded by other historians. Al-Bakri added to this information by comparing data from other people who had been there. There were, in fact, many travelers returning to Muslim Spain with different views. The Almoravids, for example, had beaten trails from several towns on the northern edge of the desert to receiving stations like Walata on the southern edge. Between northern and southern trade centers, guides directed caravans across the sands like navigators aboard ships. They marked their way by the stars and by rock formations in the desert.

Meanwhile, the fundamentalist Almoravids had pushed their way to Ghana and in the 1060s were threatening at the borders of the kingdom. For ten years, two Ghanaian kings, Bassi and Tenk Menin, defended the kingdom. But Kumbi finally fell to Muslim forces in about 1076. Al-Bakri must certainly have been aware of these happenings and gathered information from Almoravid fighters returning to Spain.

Aftermath

Ghana. The Almoravids themselves had been assembled from various North African and desert tribes (primarily the Berbers), held together only by the strong leadership of a man named al-Bakr. When he died in 1087, the power of the Almoravids collapsed. By this time, however, they had destroyed Kumbi, killed many of the Ghanaians, and forced others to swear belief in Islam. Under this weight, Ghana rapidly disintegrated, paving the way for a new empire to arise just to the south, Susu. That empire would thrive only a few years before giving way to the kingdom of Mali, and then to Songhay (Songhai). These kingdoms controlled overlapping and ever expanding regions but were effectively extensions of the old kingdom of Ghana.

Al-Bakri. The famous historian and geographer was, as were most men educated by Muslim scholars, interested in a great range of subjects. Over the course of his life, al-Bakri also assembled a collection of Arabian place names, wrote descriptions of North Africa and Moorish Spain, and produced a book about simple medicines that was still quoted as late as 1894. Al-Bakri's books on geography and history began to be published in Western Europe in about 1876.

For More Information

Chu, Daniel, and Elliott Skinner. *A Glorious Age in Africa.* Garden City, New York: Doubleday, 1965.

Davidson, Basil. *African History: Themes and Outlines.* New York: Macmillan, 1968.

Davidson, Basil, and the editors of Time-Life Books. *African Kingdoms.* New York: Time-Life Books, 1966.

McKay, John P., Bennett D. Hill, and John Buckler. *A History of World Societies.* Vol. 1. Boston: Houghton Mifflin, 1984.

Oliver, Roland, and J.D. Fage. A Short History of Africa. New York: New York University Press, 1965.

Sundiata

d. 1255

Personal Background

Sources. The story of Sundiata Keita is known only from oral accounts passed down by *griots,* the storytellers of black Africa. Numerous variations of the story of Sundiata mix legend with historical fact. In most of these stories, he appears as an almost superhuman hero.

Sundiata, which means "hungry lion," belonged to the Malinke people, also known as Mandinka or Mandingo. The Malinke were a Mandé-speaking black people in West Africa, closely related to the Soninke of Ghana and the Susa. The territory of the Malinke came to be known as Mali, meaning "where the king lives."

Heritage. Sundiata was a member of the noble Keita clan, hunters who traced their ancestry to Bilal, a black man who assisted the prophet Muhammad. The Keita clan, along with other Malinke people, had converted from paganism to Islam soon after Muslims began to penetrate West Africa in the eleventh century. Sundiata may have been born a pagan, but he was a devout Muslim by the time he became king.

Early childhood. As a very young boy, Sundiata was sickly and unable to walk. According to many oral accounts, Sundiata's father was the Malinke king, who died while Sundiata was still

▲ Sundiata

Event: The rise of Mali.

Role: After being forced into exile, Sundiata, a prince of Mali, returned to lead a successful revolt and liberate his country from Sumanguru, the king of Susu. Sundiata built a great empire by defeating Sumanguru, conquering Susu and Ghana, and then promoting trade and agriculture. He laid the foundations for an empire that would endure for centuries.

very young. He did not live to see the rise of his son, who at about the age of seven began to overcome his early handicap. Those few years of disability, however, saved him from a neighboring tyrant, Sumanguru.

Sumanguru. About 1180, the Susu, a southern branch of the Soninke tribe, formed a kingdom around the city of Susu, in what is today the Mali Republic. Eventually this kingdom fell under the power of a "warrior king born of warrior kings," Sumanguru.

In 1203 Sumanguru led an invasion of Ghana and captured its capital of Kumbi. He eventually extended his rule over all of Ghana's territory. Sumanguru ruled as a brutal tyrant. He imposed a harsh system of taxation on his subjects and made them send him large quantities of gold, food, and livestock. Sumanguru demanded that his subjects send him their most beautiful wives and daughters for his harem and their strongest and most handsome boys to be his slaves. He put to death anyone suspected of becoming a potential threat to his rule. Following the death of Sundiata's father, Sumanguru subjugated Mali, which lay to the west of Ghana. He immediately ordered the killing of Sundiata's eleven brothers to eliminate them as potential rivals. However, he spared Sundiata. Apparently he believed that the sickly, crippled child would hardly pose a threat to his power.

Sumanguru
"He was a man born to lead and command. When Sumanguru walked, he was erect as a giraffe and he was taller than all men.... And they say that the buffalo, fiercest of all animals, fled across the grasslands and hid like an old woman when Sumanguru passed" (Bertold, p. 10).

Exile. As Sundiata grew older, he overcame his earlier handicaps. Soon, he was not only walking but riding horses and hunting elephants.

Sundiata's rivals in Mali as well as Sumanguru's agents were soon plotting against him. After several attempts on his life, his mother took him into exile. They eventually settled in Mema, a kingdom on the Niger River. The king of Mema, a Muslim, hated and feared the pagan Sumanguru and welcomed the young prince and his mother. This king saw to it that Sundiata was taught leadership skills and horsemanship. In the several years that he remained in Mema, the Mali prince became an accomplished horseman and eventually commanded cavalry in Mema's army.

Participation: The Rise of Mali

Uprising. The Malinke people, meanwhile, were growing more and more uneasy under Sumanguru's rule. Finally, they sent out envoys to find Sundiata and bring him back to lead them in a revolt. By the time Sundiata was located, however, the revolt may have already begun. In 1230 the envoys at last found Sundiata and convinced him to return to Mali. There the people proclaimed him king.

Sumanguru was determined to crush the revolt. He marched into Mali at the head of a large army. The early West African kingdoms, however, were bound by the loyalties of local chiefs. In this case, the Malinke chiefs took the side of Sundiata. In addition, the king of Mema took this opportunity to try to unseat his old enemy. He sent army units that included well-trained cavalry. Near the village of Krina on the Niger, the two forces met for a decisive showdown in 1235. Sundiata's forces routed those of Sumanguru, who either fled or was killed in the fighting, depending on which oral account is considered.

Sorcery and the Battle of Krina

Kings of West Africa most often held power through claims of superiority in witchcraft. Both Sundiata and Sumanguru claimed this power, though Sundiata grew up among Muslims and had adopted that religion. Belief in the king's magical powers is illustrated in this account of the Battle of Krina:

> [Sumanguru] called upon the winds, the rain, and the earthquake. Men died like insects. Banners fell under the trampling hoofs of a thousand horses. Whole tribes were massacred in a single charge, and forests were leveled into fields. Never had men fought so savagely or so long. (Bertold, p. 30)

Expanding Mali. Sundiata established his palace at Niani, a town west of the great northern arc of the Niger River. It was an ideal location for establishing an important trading center. From there, precious gold could be sent by horse or donkey to trade centers on the southern edge of the Sahara Desert. Camel caravans from the northern desert could then trade salt and other goods for the gold and return across the desert to other centers, from which horses and donkeys could take the goods on to distribution centers along the Mediterranean Coast.

Susu and Ghana. Soon Sundiata was at war again, leading his troops against the fortified city of Susu. After a siege of several months, he captured the city and massacred the inhabitants. He then set out to conquer the rest of Sumanguru's empire. By 1240 he had captured Kumbi, the former capital of the kingdom of Ghana. According to the Arab historian Ibn Khaldun, Sundiata's troops "conquered the Susu and took over all their possessions, both their original territory and that of Ghana, as far as the ocean to the west [the Atlantic]" (Ibn Khaldun in Fage, p. 377). Sundiata proceeded to force the trading cities of Gao in the east, Djenné, and Walata to the north to pay tribute to the king (*mansa*) of *Mali*.

Consolidating the Malian empire. Following his conquests, Sundiata turned to the task of establishing a central government and restoring the region's economy. He appointed military governors to administer conquered regions. "To demonstrate their loyalty to the emperor, the governors sent gifts of rice, millet, arrows, and lances to Sundiata every year" (Chu and Skinner, p. 56). This tax was levied by the governors on all the people in their regions and by appointed rulers in the major towns and cities. Although Sundiata is said to have been a very creative ruler, this pattern of government closely followed that of the older kingdom, Ghana.

Death. According to Ibn Khaldun, Sundiata ruled for twenty-five years. During this time, he professed to be a Muslim but depended heavily on the tradition that claimed magical powers for the king. He was apparently killed in an accident in 1255. According to some accounts, he was hit by a stray arrow during a celebration; other reports say that he drowned in a river.

Aftermath

Sundiata laid the foundations of the empire of Mali, which would become the most prosperous and powerful state in West Africa. Even today, the descendants of the Malinke consider him one of their heroes. He built on Mali's strong agricultural and trade bases, establishing rules that further favored trade. After his death, Niani continued to grow as an important trade and financial center. Sundiata and his successors were able to command a great military force and build great wealth from its resources in part because of the area's large population. At its peak under **Mansa Musa** (see entry), a descendant of Sundiata who ruled from 1312 to 1337, Mali was the most powerful kingdom in Africa, with a population of eight million.

Although there is no evidence that Sundiata ever completely gave up the religious principles of the Malinke, his acceptance of Islam is borne out by events after his death. His son Uli, who ruled after him from 1255 to 1270, was a devout Muslim and the first Mali ruler to make the pilgrimage to Mecca.

For More Information

Bertold, Roland. *Sundiata: The Epic of the Lion King.* New York: Thomas Y. Crowell, 1970.

Chu, Daniel, and Elliott Skinner. *A Glorious Age in Africa.* Trenton, New Jersey: Africa World Press, 1990.

Fage, J. D., and Roland Oliver, editors. *The Cambridge History of Africa.* Vol. 3. Cambridge, England: Cambridge University Press, 1977.

Joseph, Joan. Black African Empires. New York: Franklin Watt, 1974. Levitzon, Nehemia. *Ancient Ghana and Mali.* New York: Africana Publishing, 1980.

Mansa Musa

d. c. 1332

Personal Background

King of Mali. Very little is known about the early life of Mansa Musa, which means "King Moses" in the Mandé language. He was descended from Sundiata, who is credited with establishing the Malian empire. When Musa, the grandson of one of Sundiata's sisters, assumed the throne in 1307, Mali was at the height of its power. Sundiata had conquered another great leader, Sumanguru, overrun the ancient empire of Ghana, and left his grand nephew an empire that stretched for twelve hundred miles across the grassland and desert from the Atlantic Ocean to the eastern border of present-day Nigeria.

Musa expanded this territory until its breadth across the Sahara reached beyond Timbuktu and Gao—1,600 miles from the Atlantic. He organized the many tribal groups of the area into regions—some ruled by governors (of provinces) and some controlled by vassal lords who agreed to pay homage to the great *mansa*, or king. This government of nearly eight million people was administered very efficiently. It was based on a government by regions and towns that had been used in the days of the great Ghanaian empire.

Government. This organization of *ferbas* (governors) and *mochrifs* (mayors) was so strong that it endured long after Musa died and the empire began to erode. Ibn Battutah, an Arab traveler

▲ **Mansa Musa seated on his throne at lower right.**

Event: The growth of Islam in West Africa.

Role: Mansa Musa became ruler of the kingdom of Mali long after Muslim missionaries and merchants had spread their religion throughout of West Africa. During his twenty-five-year rule, he successfully blended his people's religion, which was based on mysticism and magic, with the religion of the Mali merchant class, Islam.

who visited Mali a few years after the great mansa's death, reported that these officials kept such control that merchants could bring their caravans through Mali without fear of attack by bandits or hijackers. "[The rulers] are seldom unjust, and have a greater horror of injustice than other peoples," Ibn Battutah wrote. "There is complete serenity in their country. Neither traveler nor inhabitant have to fear robbers" (Ibn Battutah in McKay, p. 547).

It was the territories outside the king's direct control that were ruled by vassal chiefs, some of whom were appointed by him. Between thirteen and twenty-four such chiefs paid homage to Musa. To keep his vassals in line and to repel invasions, Musa maintained a huge army. It was reported that he could mount a campaign with a hundred thousand men—all well armed with spears.

The wealth of Musa. During Musa's reign the empire of Mali reached its peak and then began to decline. Nevertheless, it remained very wealthy. From his capital at Kumbi, Musa controlled the Mali economy. Farmers raised such crops as rice, beans, yams, and onions. Ranchers herded cattle, sheep, and goats. Malian miners produced copper and salt. In addition, the mansa controlled the distribution of gold mined in the independent region known as Wangara to the south (in about the middle of the Senegal River basin). The power at Kumbi controlled trade from along the Atlantic coast and across the Sahara Desert. Gold was gathered in the south, brought to Kumbi, and then sent to Timbuktu, the shipping center of the Muslims on the edge of the Sahara Desert. There it was traded for salt from such communities as Taghaza in the central desert. At the time of Musa, Mali was the main source of Europe's gold. Of course, Musa demanded taxes or tributes of everyone who traded in his empire and as a result grew to be very rich.

Timbuktu and Gao. Some historians credit Musa or his generals with conquering Timbuktu and Gao, other centers of commerce and culture, but these locales may have already been part of the Malian empire by the time Musa became king. Mali did become a center of culture and learning during Musa's reign. Particularly after he made a visit to the great cities of Cairo and Mecca, the mansa encouraged teaching and scholarly study at the

▲ A fourteenth-century mosque in Djenné, Mali; Mansa Musa successfully blended the Malian people's religion, which was based on mysticism and magic, with Islam.

University of Sankoré in Timbuktu. The university attracted scholars from all over Africa and the Muslim world.

Participation:
The Growth of Islam in West Africa

Islam and black African traditions. Much of the interest in trade, as well as the stimulation to study, had been brought to West Africa by Muslims. It was Muslim traders, the Almoravids, following the coastline from Morocco southward, who built the caravan stop at Timbuktu and who earlier had dominated governments in the region. Long before Musa became king, Islam was well accepted by merchants and rulers, though the average West African clung to more ancient religious traditions often centered around kings who claimed mystical and magical powers. Rulers before Musa had claimed Islam as their religion; some had even made the pilgrimage to Mecca. But since their power to rule was, in the eyes of the people, based on magical abilities, it was difficult for Musa and the previous kings to completely abandon their traditional cultural beliefs. The mix of Islam and paganism became very conspicuous when, in 1324, Musa decided to make his own pilgrimage.

The hajj. Musa used his trip to the holy city of Mecca not only to show his subservience to the God of Islam but also to demonstrate his own importance as ruler of an enormously wealthy trading state. Instead of joining a caravan and traveling humbly as was the case with most makers of the *hajj* (holy excursion to Mecca), Musa chose to travel lavishly. Part of this demonstration was to impress the ruler of Egypt, to whom Musa planned a state visit.

Leaving his son in Niani, the Malian capital city, to reign in his absence, Musa departed for Mecca, taking with him doctors, teachers, important chiefs, and thousands of followers. To finance the *hajj,* the caravan included a great herd of pack animals. Some accounts tell of eighty to one hundred camels with loads of gold dust each weighing about 300 pounds. (In 1995 this much gold would have been worth about $200 million.) Other accounts tell of a hundred elephants each carrying one hundred pounds of gold.

Several hundred more camels carried food, supplies, and weapons. Five hundred slaves marched before the king, each carrying a six-pound gold staff.

Cairo. In July 1324 the caravan reached Cairo, where Musa was elaborately entertained by the sultan of Egypt. Other foreign visitors were required to kneel before the sultan and kiss the ground. But Musa considered himself a superior foreign dignitary. After all, Mali was larger and more powerful than Egypt at that time. He refused to kneel and, at the same time, declared his loyalty to Islam, proclaiming, "I will prostrate myself before Allah who created me and brought me into the world" (Davidson, p. 84). A second visit to Cairo.

Musa then proceeded to Mecca but stopped again in Cairo on his return trip. He gave presents of gold to government officials and spent more gold shopping in the Cairo markets. In fact, he put so much gold into circulation in Egypt that the value of the Egyptian currency fell. And despite all the gold he brought with him, Musa was so generous in his gift-giving that he ran out of money and had to borrow from Cairo merchants to finance his return trip.

Return home. During his pilgrimage, Musa met the famous Arab poet and architect as-Saheli and persuaded him to accompany the caravan back to Mali. As-Saheli would later design mosques in Timbuktu and Gao as well as Musa's royal palace.

On the way home, Musa made a side trip to Gao, about 350 miles south and east of Timbuktu. Gao was the capital of the kingdom of Songhay, a vassal state of Mali. Musa abducted the king of Songhay's two sons and took them home with him. One of them, Ali Kolon, would become a military commander in Musa's army.

Musa received a warm welcome once back in Niani. Still, this welcome had little to do with his newly reinforced commitment to Islam. The citizens of Mali continued to recognize him as a wise man and a clever magician.

Aftermath

Islam and Timbuktu. After his pilgrimage, Musa became more dedicated to the Islamic religion. He turned his attention to

▲ **A Malian clay fortification; Mansa Musa hired Muslim engineers to replace Timbuktu's pounded clay permanent structures with brick.**

Timbuktu, a stop for caravans crossing the desert. He hired Muslim engineers to replace the pounded-clay structures in the village with brick, and as-Saheli was commissioned to build several mosques in the growing city. Musa raised Timbuktu to a center of Muslim intellectual activity. There were 150 colleges dedicated to the study of Islam, and a school of Islamic law became the most impressive law center in Africa. The city also became the hub of a vigorous book-selling industry that introduced Islam to the Haas people south of Mali and Songhay. A great store of judges, doctors, priests, and other scholars began to gather in Timbuktu to study and seek the sponsorship of the king.

Mali. Musa's trip to the Holy Land had acquainted him with the Mediterranean powers, and as a result, he made trade alliances with Morocco and Egypt. Because the rulers of these countries were Muslims, he continued to encourage the growth of Islam in Mali, persuading his traders to wear flowing robes and turbans like their trading partners. Stories of the wealth of the mansa spread to Europe. Map makers began to put Mali on the map, and European and North African rulers began to recognize it as a great empire. Mali would remain the chief source of gold for Europe until explorers Hernando Cortés and Francisco Pizarro found their own sources in the Americas.

By the time of Musa's death, which is considered to have occurred around 1332, Mali had reached the peak of its greatness and had begun a long and gradual decline. The great mansa was succeeded by a series of weak and incompetent rulers. Shortly after his death, Mossi people from the Volta River valley captured Timbuktu, and it began to lose its lustre. The two princes that he had brought back from Songhay escaped and returned home to found a new dynasty. Songhay soon gained its independence from Mali and would become one of the most powerful states in West Africa. Mali would decline for nearly two centuries before being absorbed into Songhay.

For More Information

Chu, Daniel, and Elliott Skinner. *A Glorious Age in Africa.* Trenton, New Jersey: Africa World Press, 1990.

Davidson, Basil, and the editors of Time-Life Books. *African Kingdoms.* New York: Time, 1966.

McKay, John P., Bennett D. Hill, and John Buckler. *A History of World Societies.* Vol. 1. Boston: Houghton Mifflin, 1984.

Murphy, E. Jefferson. *History of African Civilization.* New York: Delta Publishing, 1972.

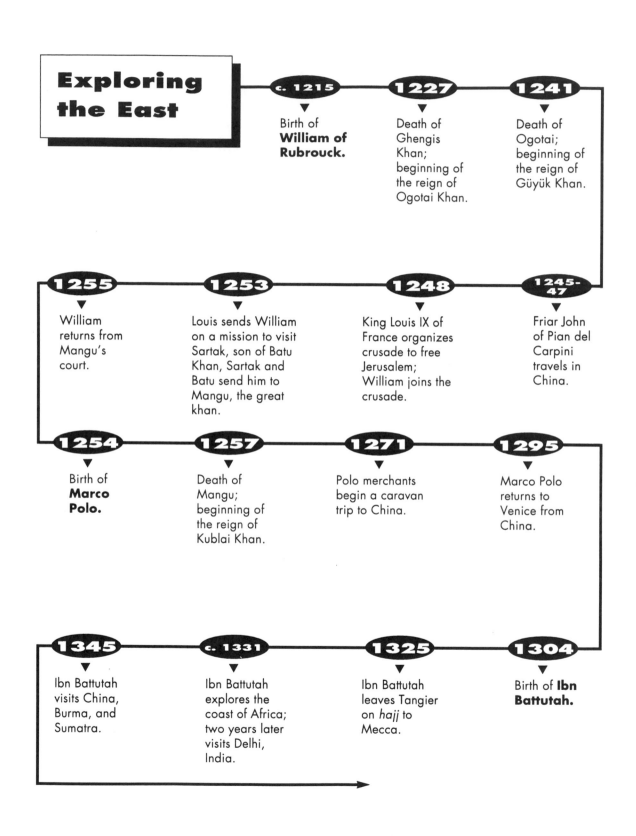

Exploring the East

c. 1215 ▼ Birth of **William of Rubrouck.**

1227 ▼ Death of Ghengis Khan; beginning of the reign of Ogotai Khan.

1241 ▼ Death of Ogotai; beginning of the reign of Güyük Khan.

1255 ▼ William returns from Mangu's court.

1253 ▼ Louis sends William on a mission to visit Sartak, son of Batu Khan, Sartak and Batu send him to Mangu, the great khan.

1248 ▼ King Louis IX of France organizes crusade to free Jerusalem; William joins the crusade.

1245-47 ▼ Friar John of Pian del Carpini travels in China.

1254 ▼ Birth of **Marco Polo.**

1257 ▼ Death of Mangu; beginning of the reign of Kublai Khan.

1271 ▼ Polo merchants begin a caravan trip to China.

1295 ▼ Marco Polo returns to Venice from China.

1345 ▼ Ibn Battutah visits China, Burma, and Sumatra.

c. 1331 ▼ Ibn Battutah explores the coast of Africa; two years later visits Delhi, India.

1325 ▼ Ibn Battutah leaves Tangier on *hajj* to Mecca.

1304 ▼ Birth of **Ibn Battutah.**

EXPLORING
THE EAST

The Crusades. **T**he Crusades that began in the eleventh century A.D. and continued into the fifteenth century triggered the beginning of an age of exploration. Crusaders traveling to Constantinople (the capital of the Greek Orthodox (Christian) Byzantine Empire—today it's known as Istanbul) became acquainted with traders from far-off countries and wondered at their unfamiliar dress and customs. Western traders, or their part, eagerly set out to explore and learn about the great countries of the East in the hope of sharing in the region's great wealth of goods and gold.

Alexander, Nestorians, and Islam. For the Western world, it was a time of awakening to the little-known East, which had been known since Alexander the Great marched into India in 326 B.C., though it had never been fully explored. In the fifth century, Christianity, still in its early stages, acted as an impetus for travel eastward. Debates about the nature of the new religion created friction and drove some Christians from the church at Constantinople. These exiled Christians, who followed a leader named Nestorius, headed east into Asia to avoid persecution. There they created Christian settlements, which relayed information about the region back to the West. Then, in the seventh century, a new religion, Islam, began to spread its teachings throughout the world. Islamic settlements sprang up in India and

▲ **Fourteenth-century miniature of Marco Polo entering Beijing (Peking).**

as far away as the coast of China (the religion was based in the Middle East). And by the eleventh century, the Christian crusaders, also eager to spread their religion, had begun to head east. Thus the age of exploration was stimulated by religious fervor from both Islam and Christianity.

Mongols. Meanwhile, an equally curious and aggressive people were exploring northern Asia. By the early thirteenth century, the Mongols had united to form one of the world's most formidable armies and had marched across Mongolia to attack Persia in the west and China in the east and south.

Westerners went to live among the Mongols for many reasons: to spread their religions, to take advantage of new trade outlets, out of curiosity, or just to establish a life away from the contentious civilizations of Europe. One of the earliest European travelers to the East, Rabbi Benjamin, lived in China from 1160 to 1173. Friar John Carpini visited China in an attempt to convert people to Christianity as early as 1245. He was not the only European there. Already, the Mongols had taken Europeans as servants and slaves, and some European craftsmen were later discovered as part of the Mangu Khan's court.

Explorers. Three men stand out as explorers who provided the world with accurate accounts of the geography, populations, and cultures of the East. **William of Rubrouck** visited the palace of Mangu Khan in 1253 to win converts to Christianity. Though he was evicted from China by the khan, he returned from Asia to write a clear and concise account of his experiences for France's king, Louis IX, who had sponsored William's trip.

Marco Polo, a trader from Venice, Italy, visited Kublai Khan in 1275 on a trading mission. Unlike Rubrouck, however, he made himself of so much use to the khan that he, his father, and his uncle were not allowed to leave China for seventeen years.

In 1325 a Moroccan named **Ibn Battutah** traveled thousands of miles east to complete the pilgrimage to Mecca required of all Muslims. After returning home, he set out on another journey that lasted thirty years and covered more than seventy thousand miles through Syria, Persia, Arabia, the African coast, and North and West Africa.

William, Polo, and Ibn Battutah were not the first European or African explorers in Asia, nor were they the most successful in accomplishing their goals. They stand out in history because of the written accounts they produced of their travels. From these accounts, Europeans developed accurate maps of the East, and their maps and stories inspired other explorers. One of those for whom the work of Polo and William was particularly important was Christopher Columbus.

Mongol exploration. And Europeans were certainly not the only people with adventurous spirits and curiosity about the world. Mongol leaders frequently pursued possibilities that promised to bring peace and unity to an ever-growing and diversifying population. Mongol representatives visited Christian centers in Europe and invited people of the Christian and Islamic worlds to visit Asia and teach their traditions. Under Mongol rule, Chinese shipbuilders and explorers visited much of the territory around the Indian Ocean and beyond.

Marco Polo

1254-1324

Personal Background

Early life. Marco Polo was born into a moderately successful Venice merchant family in 1254. The Polo family was of Dalma-
tian heritage (with family ties to the coastal area later known as
Yugoslavia), but Marco's father and uncles lived and traded in
Venice, where Marco was born. Polo's father, Nicolo, was away on
business when the boy was born, and shortly after the birth,
Polo's mother died. Still, there was plenty of family around to see
to the upbringing of the baby boy. Marco lived with his Aunt Flora
until his father's return to Venice fifteen years later.

The Polos' trading business sometimes took them as far
away as Constantinople, the capital of the Greek Orthodox (Christian) Byzantine Empire. Just before Marco was born, Nicolo and
Marco's Uncle Maffeo were sent on business to Constantinople.
They stayed there for six years and then decided to travel into the
land of the Mongols, driven by stories of the great wealth of the
various rulers, known as khans.

At that time, the empire of Genghis Khan was beginning to
break down. Genghis had divided his realm among his sons. He
appointed one of them, Ogotai, to serve as the ruler of Mongolia
and therefore as the khan of khans. By the time the Polo brothers
arrived in Mongolia, Kublai was the great khan. Nicolo and Maffeo stayed in Karakorum, the capital city of the Mongolian

▲ Marco Polo

Event: Western exploration of the East.

Role: In 1271 Marco Polo, son of a Venetian merchant, went with his father and uncle on a trading mission to Constantinople. They returned after nearly twenty-five years, having traveled as far as the summer and winter palaces of Kublai Khan, the emperor of China. Two years later, Polo dictated a narrative of his adventures that described major cities and peoples of the East.

empire, for seven years before returning to Europe. They had found Kublai greatly interested in Christianity and had been sent home to deliver a request of the pope.

Kublai had become alarmed by the crudeness of his fellow Mongols and at their tendency to battle one another. He had listened to Christian missionaries and decided that their religion might be one way to teach more peaceful ways to his subjects. He asked the pope to send one hundred missionaries to China to teach the people there. Unfortunately, the Polo brothers returned to Italy to find that the pope they had befriended had died and there was as yet no replacement. They then went home to Venice, where Nicolo learned that his wife had also died—and that he had a fifteen-year-old son. Marco had received little formal education, though it is believed that he did learn to read and write. Life in Venice was centered on trade and on the Catholic Church. In fact, the boy had been named after the patron saint of Venice. Marco had probably spent much time attending religious festivals and hearing stories of the saints and prophets. Other than that, little is known of his childhood.

Participation:
A Western Exploration of the East

Travel to Cathay. In their seven-year stay with Kublai, Nicolo and Maffeo had learned the Mongol language. They had also seen the riches of the khan and of the trade in his empire. As merchants, they were not willing to give up the opportunities of the East. Soon after they returned to Venice, the brothers began to plan a second trip, this time to Cathay (China). They planned to take Marco with them, but before they left, Nicolo and Maffeo wanted to meet as many of the great khan's requests as they could. He had asked for a vial of holy oil, for which the brothers had to travel to Jerusalem. They also obtained a letter from a high-ranking Church official assuring the khan that a new pope would try to satisfy his request for missionaries. It was two years before the Polos were ready to return to Kublai's palace.

The three Polos sailed from Venice to Acre (in present-day Israel) in 1271 and organized a caravan. That year they left Acre

▲ **The Polos setting out with their caravan to Cathay; the trip would take one year and three months to complete.**

with a well-supplied caravan. The journey took them to Hormuz in the Persian Gulf and north to Khorasan in northern Persia (now Iran), then across the northern steppes to Afghanistan and over the mountains to Khotan in China. From there they crossed the Gobi Desert to the khan's summer palace at Kaipungfu in Mongolia. The trip had taken one year and three months to complete. All along the way, Marco took careful notice of the countryside and the people.

Adventures along the way. The travelers had encountered many obstacles on their trip. Polo later included the tales of his first journey in a book. He recounted that the three merchants had intended to sail from Hormuz to China but found that the ships available there had been built without nails and thus did not seem seaworthy. The poor food and curious customs of the Muslim people in Hormuz left a burning impression on young Marco.

In northeastern Persia the Polos encountered bandits called Karaunas who attacked the caravan with such force that only ten

▲ **Kublai Khan; Marco Polo made himself of so much use to the khan that he, his father, and his uncle were not allowed to leave China for seventeen years.**

of the traveling men escaped, by fleeing to a village nearby. Other members of the caravan were killed or carried off to be sold as slaves. In northern Afghanistan, the Polos traveled to the ancient city of Balkh, which had once been the glorious capital of a country called Bactria. They found it a blackened ruin, for years before Ghengis Khan had burned the city to the ground, ordering the elderly put to death and the young sold as slaves. In Badakhshan, near the Oxus river, Marco began to see evidence of the wealth of the region. Mines there yielded rubies, sapphires, and lapis lazuli. But Marco also remembered the place because he had become ill there. On the advice of local residents, the caravan moved up the mountains to find streams of fresh water and abundant fish. There they rested before crossing Afghanistan and the Gobi Desert to reach their destination in 1275.

At the palace. Perhaps Marco had learned some of the Mongolian language along the way, for he soon impressed the khan. The early author Pipino wrote:

> [Marco] learned the uses of the Tatars and their language and their letters and their archery so well that it seemed a wonder to them all, for I tell you quite truly that before a great deal of time after he came to the court of the great lord, he knows several languages and four other different letters and writings so that he could read and write in any of those languages very well. (Hart, p. 125)

Kublai decided to test Marco by sending him as a messenger to cities in China. The first mission was to Caragian (Qara-Jang) in the south of China, a journey that required six months of travel. Polo returned and reported what he had learned to the khan in such detail that those around the court began to revere him as a great man.

Marco remained in the service of the great khan for nearly seventeen years. At one time, he was made governor of one of the large Chinese cities. And his travels for the khan allowed him to study the geography and people of many other places in Asia— either through personal visits or by hearing the accounts of other travelers.

Return to Venice. Over the years, Marco became indispensable to Kublai—or so the khan apparently thought. Over and over the Polos asked for and were deprived of the freedom to return to Venice. Once, when Nicolo begged on his knees for freedom to go home, Kublai said that there was no condition in the world that would make him willing to let them depart. But at last the khan's trust in Marco gave him and his family their opportunity.

The wife of a lesser khan, Argon Khan of Persia, grand-nephew of Kublai, had died. Argon sent three ambassadors to his great uncle's palace to request that a replacement be sent. It was an easy request for the old khan to fill, for he was accustomed to gathering one hundred of the fairest maidens of the land each year for his own uses. In this case he knew of the perfect choice—Kuchachin (Cocacin) was seventeen, beautiful, pleasant tempered, and from a good family. She would be sent as the new bride of this favorite lesser khan. A great band of Argon's followers assembled to accompany Kuchachin over the land route to Persia. They were well on their way to Persia when the band was caught in a war among northern Tatar tribes. After eight months, the convoy was forced to return to the palace at Cambaluc (Beijing).

Marco Polo and the Women of Hangchow

The early author Ramusio wrote of Marco Polo's vision of the women of China: "And their ladies and wives are also most delicate and angelique things, and raised gently, and with great delicacy, and they clothe themselves with so many ornaments of silk and of jewels, that the value of them cannot be estimated" (Hart, p. 135).

The Polos took advantage of the problem. They persuaded the khan that it would be safer to send the girl by sea, and even safer if they escorted her since the Polos were experienced travelers in Persia and Marco could speak some of the languages. Kublai was unhappy, but the prospective marriage was important, for gifts of wives was one way to cement relationships among the khans. In the end he agreed, even though the agreement would release the Polos to go home.

Fourteen ships were fitted out in a port in southern China and the expedition set sail. This trip stopped at many places and gave Marco the opportunity to make more notes about the geography and the peoples of Asia. One of the stops was in the country of Champa (Vietnam), where Marco had earlier noted there was a king with 326 children, 150 of them men capable of bearing arms. They also stopped at the island of Java, at Ceylon, and at Malabar in India. Everywhere they went, Marco Polo found something

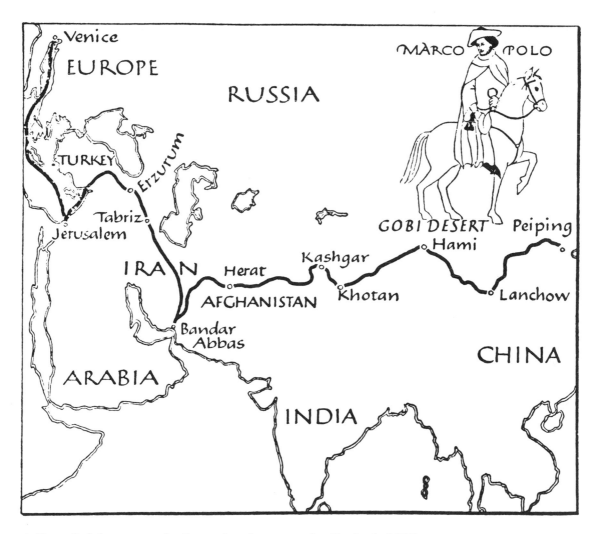

Map labels: Venice, EUROPE, RUSSIA, MARCO POLO, TURKEY, Erzurum, Tabriz, Jerusalem, IRAN, Herat, AFGHANISTAN, Kashgar, Khotan, GOBI DESERT, Hami, Peiping, Lanchow, CHINA, Bandar Abbas, ARABIA, INDIA

▲ Marco Polo's route to the East; when he returned to Venice in 1295 with tales of faraway peoples and places, some people thought that his stories could not be true.

marvelous or amazing. In one place, sailors were not allowed to testify in court; in another, religious celebrations involved both young men and women dancing naked at the temples. In still another, the people all worshipped Buddha, whom Marco felt must be one of the greatest of teachers.

The party visited Madagascar and the coast of Africa (Ethiopia), and returned to Hormuz, now a swarming port city trading in Asian spices, peppers, dates, sandalwood, and rice. At

Hormuz, they learned that Argon had died. Other arrangements had to be made for Kuchachin. After consultation with Argon's brother, it was decided to give the prospective bride to Argon's son, Ghazan (Casan). He was at war on the Khorasan border, and that required another trip by the Polos. This mission accomplished, the travelers went to Tabriz, organized a caravan there, and finally worked their way back to Venice. They had been gone nearly twenty-five years. No traveler had ever visited more places in Asia than Marco, now in his forties.

Aftermath

Welcome home. Marco returned to Venice in 1295, wearing the simple clothing of the Mongols and filled with tales of faraway peoples and places. The people of Venice were divided in their reactions to him. Some thought his stories so strange that they could not possibly be true. Others wondered if he even was the real Marco Polo who had left on a merchant trip twenty-five years earlier. Soon, however, the people of Venice were convinced. Marco's reputation and the riches he had brought from Asia made him an important person in the city. He was given the nickname Marco Millioni. He settled into the life of a man of wealth and married a woman named Donata, with whom he would have three daughters: Fantina, Bellela, and Moreta. In Venice, however, wealth and respect brought responsibilities.

Venice was at war with its commercial competitor Genoa, and it was the duty of wealthy men to build and man ships for the war. Marco had a galley built and became the ship's captain. Unfortunately for Venice, Genoa was the stronger of the two cities. In one great naval battle in 1298, the Venetians were defeated and seven

The Polos Teach the Khan About Warfare

One story tells how Kublai, in his constant struggle to subdue all of China, besieged the city of Saianfu. The siege lasted for three years without success. Nicolo, Maffeo, and Marco told the khan they could show him a way to force the city to surrender:

> Great Prince, we have with us among our followers men who are able to construct mangonels which shall cast such great stones that the garrison will never be able to stand them, but will surrender incontinently, as soon as the mangonels or trebuchets shall have shot into the town. (Marco Polo quoted in Tappan, pp. 119-20)

The machines were built and used. The city surrendered, and Kublai Khan was introduced to the European catapult.

thousand of their sailors taken captive, including Marco, who would remain in prison for two years. His cellmate in prison was Rustichello of Pisa, a skilled writer. To pass the time, Rustichello agreed that he would write the story if Marco would dictate an account of his trip to Asia. The resulting book, *The Book of Marco Polo Concerning the Kingdoms and Marvels of the East,* gained little respect at first. People felt that the stories were too wild to be true. But one man, Roger Bacon, seemed to recognize the value of the book and used it as a reference for his own work. Later, another world traveler, Christopher Columbus, would consider the book's excellent geographical descriptions in reaching his decision to try for Asia by sailing across the Atlantic Ocean.

For More Information

Hart, Henry H. *Marco Polo: Venetian Adventurer.* Norman: University of Oklahoma Press, 1967.

Komroff, Manuel, editor. *Contemporaries of Marco Polo.* New York: Liveright, 1928.

Mote, F. W., editor. *The Travels of Marco Polo.* New York: McGraw Hill, 1961.

Tappan, Eva March, editor. *The World's Story: A History of the World in Story, Song and Art.* Vol. 1. Boston: Riverside Press, 1914.

William of Rubrouck

c. 1215-c. 1295

Personal Background

Early record. It seems certain that William of Rubrouck was born in the town of Rubrouck near Saint Omer, France, in the year 1215. At an early age, he apparently decided to join the ministry and took up studies to become a Franciscan monk (a member of the order founded by St. Francis). Otherwise, very little is known about his early life, except that he grew to be a very pious young man and also grew to be a bit stout. His deep religious beliefs gave him a strong will and a light heart that were later revealed in his writing. Even in the face of formidable foes, he was able to speak up for what he saw as the right course.

Louis IX. Louis IX, the king of France, was also a pious man and so strong a champion of Christianity that he would later be named a saint. In 1248 he began to organize a crusade to regain the rule of Jerusalem for Christians. Louis gathered fifty thousand armed men in a short time and marched off to win the holy city. Friar William of Rubrouck saw this as an opportunity to serve Christianity and decided to go along with Louis.

The mission, however, was unsuccessful, for Jerusalem could not be taken. The great procession was returning from its expedition when Louis heard that Sartak, son of Batu, the Mongol khan of Russia, had become a Christian. Louis thought that if this were true, there would be great opportunities to advance the reli-

▲ **The Buddhist Temple of One Thousand Lamas in Tibet; William of Rubrouck was the first Westerner to describe the lamas of Tibet.**

Event: Visiting the great khan Mangu.

Role: After joining Louis IX, king of France, on an ill-fated crusade to recover Jerusalem, William of Rubrouck was sent by the king to spread Christianity in the East. Louis had heard that the son of Batu, khan of Russia, had become a Christian and wanted to confirm his friendly relations with the Church. The journey eventually led William to visit the great khan at the Mongolian capital Karakorum—a trip of more than ten thousand miles.

gion in Russia. Louis ordered William to go to the palace of Sartak and Batu to learn the truth. The faithful monk received this order at Acre, in what is now Israel. He immediately set out for Constantinople, capital of the Greet Orthodox (Christian) Byzantine Empire.

Participation: Visiting Mangu, the Great Khan

At the khan's ordu. By William's time the great Mongolian empire of Genghis Khan was beginning to break apart. There was still a supreme commander, the great khan, who made his headquarters in Karakorum. But the empire was divided among the khan's relatives, each of whom ruled a part of the territory with very little interference from the great khan. Thus, when Batu was khan of Russia, a small part of his empire was ruled by his eldest son, Sartak. These two often shared an *ordu*, or a temporary camp, as they moved their herds north in the summer and south in the winter.

William left Constantinople on May 7, 1253, carrying letters to Batu from Louis and from Baldwin II, the last Roman emperor headquartered in the East. The friar and a four-strong band of followers, including one servant, would sail to the Crimea and then travel overland north and east to find the ordu of Sartak and Batu. Two weeks of sailing across the Black Sea brought the group to a port city called Soldaia (now Sudak). They debated whether to make the rest of the journey on horseback or by wagon. Other travelers in Constantinople had advised them to take covered wagons to protect their property and to avoid continued loading and unloading at campsites. William decided on the wagons but later regretted it. The oxen pulling the wagons traveled at a more gentle pace so that, he said, "I was traveling to Sartak two months which I could have done in one had I gone by horse" (Komroff, p. 57).

On the journey to Sartak, the five travelers found themselves in a strange world. Here the residents did not live in cities but carried their felt-and-pole homes with them on great carts drawn by large harnesses of oxen. William noted that some of the carts were twenty feet wide and some of the houses were wider than

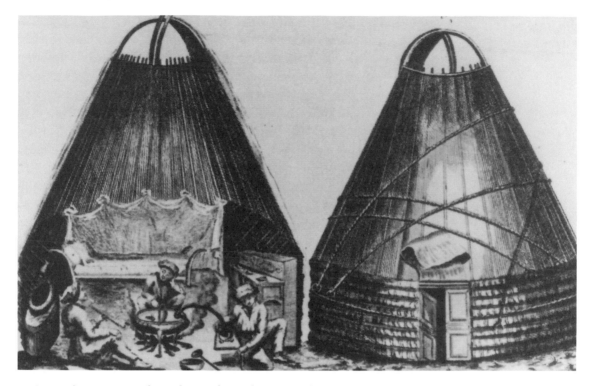

▲ An ancient yurt, or domed tent, from the Mongolian steppes; most Mongols carried their felt-and-pole homes with them on great carts drawn by large harnesses of oxen.

the carts by as much as five feet on each side. Girls drove the oxen pulling the carts; one girl, he noted, was driving twenty or thirty carts lashed together.

With Sartak. The Christian party reached the ordu of Sartak where the city of Saratov now stands. They rode with Sartak's people for four days. According to his account of the trip, William was interrogated and mistreated the whole time. "The bishop of this church [St. Sophia] had been to Sartak, and he told me many good things concerning [Sartak], which later I failed to discover for myself" (William in Komroff, p. 56). One of the disappointments was that Sartak would not admit to having become a Christian. William was also dismayed by Sartak's lack of courtesy; he was willing to accept gifts, but he did not give gifts in return.

Batu. After the four days, Sartak ordered the Christians to travel to the ordu of his father Batu. Arriving at Batu's camp on the eastern side of the Volga River, William began a five-week tour of the area. When he finally was allowed an audience with the khan, they talked of religion and of the reason for the visit. To show his pleasure at their visit, Batu drank milk with them. Soon after this meeting, a messenger of the khan explained that Batu would like them to remain in his land but that it was not his decision to make. The Christians must travel to the great khan Mangu and seek his permission. It was a trip of more than five thousand miles, which William would have to make on horseback because Sartak had demanded that he leave the four wagons with him. On September 16, 1253, William and his band left the court of Batu and headed east. Their destination was Karakorum, the original capital of the Mongols and the place where Mangu Khan held court.

William traveled north of the Caspian and Aral seas. He crossed the Ural River on the twelfth day. His journey took him south to Tibet, then east through China and finally north to the great plain of Mongolia. Along the way, the friar surveyed the land and the people and wrote an account of the great cities, temples, and castles he saw. He also encountered traditions that he thought strange: the habit of the people of Tangut to attack anyone dressed in red; the Tibetan custom of eating the flesh of one's dead parents; and the tendency (which was totally unacceptable to William) of Nestorians (a sect of Christians who had lived in the East for hundreds of years) to live among and deal with Saracens (Muslims).

Inside a Mongol Home

At a campsite, the men unloaded the houses from the carts. It was left to the women to organize the houses and provide meals for the men. All houses faced to the south, and men and women occupied designated spots inside, the male master on the north, women on the east, and men on the west. William wrote of this arrangement:

> Over the master's head is always an image, like a puppet, made of felt, which they call the master's brother: and another over the head of the good wife or mistress, which they call her brother, is fastened to the wall: and higher up between both of them, there is a little lean one, which is as it were the guardian of the whole house.
> (William in Komroff, p. 61)

Crossing a portion of Cathay (China), the band had its first experience with Buddhism, noting monks who served "idols," (most likely statues of Buddha). William wrote, "The priests of the idols of these people wear large yellow coloured hoods.... [Some] live very austere lives in the woods" (William in Komroff, p. 120).

In this region, William took pains to identify Christian communities—there were fifteen cities of Nestorians. Heading north from China across more mountains, William's band reached Mangu's court in late 1253. There they were surprised to find a Hungarian servant who recognized their Catholic order (Franciscan), a Nestorian Christian who was an adviser to the great khan, an Armenian monk, and a silversmith from Paris. There were also several other Europeans at the court, most of them having been taken as prisoners and made servants of the khan.

Religious debates and the Khan. William remained as a guest of the khan for nearly five months. In that time, representatives of the other religions found in Karakorum, Nestorians and Saracens among them, initiated debates with this man who claimed to understand the will of God. After a while, news of these debates reached the khan, along with word that William thought his host a sinner. Mangu then invited all the believers in one God to come before him and present their views about God's will.

The friar responded that he was not in competition with the other religions but would nonetheless be happy to express his religious beliefs in the spirit of love. Evidently, by then Mangu had had enough of this friar. He summoned William and ordered him to leave his land.

The return trip. Around July 10, 1254, William's party left Mangu to return to Batu carrying warlike messages from Mangu to Pope John with instructions that they be edited by the lesser khan.

> ### The Nestorians
>
> A great debate took place early in the history of Christianity over the real place of Jesus Christ. Some believed God was twofold: a Holy Spirit and Christ, the physical form of God. Others believed that Christ was not God, but the son and messenger of God. The Nestorians of the fifth century A.D. believed in a single God in two forms, physical and spiritual. For their beliefs, they were driven away from other Christians. They established their own communities in Persia, Afghanistan, and China.

This time, they took a more northerly route to the ordu of Batu, who reviewed the great khan's messages. It was now November, and sailing across the Black Sea was impossible in winter. They thus traveled overland along the Caucasus Mountains and across Turkey, finally arriving on the island of Cyprus. From there, the party traveled to Tripoli in northern Africa, arriving after thirteen months of travel on August 15, 1255. This return trip, winding its

143

▲ The Erdeni-Tsu monastery in Mongolia, southwest of Ulan-Bator; William of Rubrouck was the first European to visit Christian communities in Mongolia.

way north and then south, was considerably longer than the five thousand-mile trip to visit Mangu Khan.

As part of his original mission, William was to bring to Louis a report of the lands through which he had passed and of the peoples he had encountered. William had hoped to report to the king at Acre, where Louis had established headquarters. But when he arrived in Acre, he learned that Louis had returned to France a year earlier. So the friar entered a monastery in Acre and spent two years writing a factual report of what he had seen and heard, with an occasional comment on his opinions. The report revealed that William had learned the Chinese writing symbols, thus becoming the first European to do so. He had also been the first to visit Christian communities in Mongolia and the first to describe the lamas (religious leaders) of Tibet.

Aftermath

After writing his report, William disappeared from history. The year of his death is still in dispute; some historians say 1295; others say 1270. Nevertheless, William's work lives on. A fellow Franciscan, Roger Bacon, found William's account of his travels and used many of his descriptions in a geographical section of a book he was preparing. And in the days before printed books, William's *Journal of Friar William of Rubrouck: A Frenchman of the Order of the Minor Friars, to the East Parts of the World, in the Years 1253 to 1255* was copied in manuscript form several times. Five of these manuscripts still exist in Cambridge, England, and Leiden in the Netherlands. The book was not printed until 1598.

The Palace of Mangu Khan

"There is a palace there [Karakorum] where [the Great Khan] gives a great feast twice a year, at Easter when he passes through, and in summer when he leaves.... At the entrance of this great palace—for it would not seem fit to bring there goat-skin bottles of milk or other drinks—master William of Paris placed a great silver tree, at the foot of which are four silver lions having a spout and all pouring forth mare's white milk.... The palace is like a church having a nave in the center and two side aisles separated from the nave by two rows of pillars." (William in Komroff, pp. 157-58)

For More Information

Curtin, Jeremiah. *Mongols: A History.* New York: Greenwood, 1973.

Komroff, Manuel. *Contemporaries of Marco Polo.* New York: Horace Liveright, 1928.

Morgan, David. *Mongols.* New York: Blackwell, 1987.

Ibn Battutah

1304-c. 1368

Personal Background

Early life. Ibn Battutah was born in Tangier on February 25, 1304. His full name was Abu Abdullah Muhammad ibn 'Abdallah ibn Muhammad ibn Ibrahim al-Lawati ibn Battutah. His father was descended from a Berber tribe, the Lawata. Several members of his family were Muslim legal scholars, and he adhered to that tradition, studying law as a young man. He is thought to have received the finest legal education available in Tangier, though the quality of that education is in dispute as Ibn Battutah had apparently completed his studies before he was twenty-one.

Much of what is known about Ibn Battutah comes from his own writings, and these carry little reference to his early life. Manuscripts he wrote in later life begin in the year 1325 when he was twenty-one years old; that is when the adventurous and religious young man decided to strike out on a pilgrimage to Mecca.

Participation: Exploring the Muslim World

The hajj. The dangers of traveling across northern Africa at that time were great. A single traveler was likely to encounter bands of robbers all along the way. So most people interested in making the pilgrimage gathered in small groups on the road from Fez (Morocco) to Tlemcen (Algeria) to form a large and protective caravan. But Ibn Battutah left Tangier on June 14, 1325, to

▲ Ibn Battutah

Event: Exploring the Muslim world.

Role: Ibn Battutah, a Muslim legal student from Tangier, decided at age twenty-one to make the *hajj,* the Islamic pilgrimage to Mecca. Striking out alone, he traveled through Egypt, Palestine, and Syria. After this adventure, he made several other excursions by land and ship, visiting most of the Islamic world of his time. After twenty-four years of exploration, he returned to his native Tangier, where he recorded his experiences.

make his way to Mecca alone. His path took him along the coast of North Africa to Alexandria, Egypt, a distance of more than two thousand miles.

Troubles began almost immediately. At Bijaya the young traveler became ill with such a fever that he was advised to stay in the city to rest. But Ibn Battutah was determined. "If God decrees my death, then my death shall be on the road, with my face set towards the land of [Mecca]," he responded (Ibn Battutah in Dunn, p. 33). Then, in the beautiful port city of Tunis, he watched as a *shaykh* (religious ruler) and a *qadi* (judge) were welcomed to the city. For the first time in his travels, he felt lonely:

> I felt so sad at heart on account of my loneliness that I could not restrain the tears that started to my eyes, and wept bitterly.... One of the pilgrims, realizing the cause of my distress, came up to me with a greeting and friendly welcome, and continued to comfort me with friendly talk until I entered the city, where I lodged at the college of the Booksellers. (Ibn Battutah in Dunn, p. 37)

Cities on the Route of Ibn Battutah's First *Hajj*

Following is a list of present-day cities on the route of Ibn Battutah's first *hajj:*

Abadan	Faid	Shiraz
Alexandria	Isfahan	Sousa
Algiers	Kazarum	Surt
Annaba	Kufah	Tabriz
Aydhab	Mecca	Tangier
Baghdad	Medina	Tlemcen
Basra	Miliana	Tripoli
Bijaya	Mosul	Tunis
Cairo	Qabis	Wasit
Damascus	Qus	

Marriage. He soon found a way to remedy this loneliness, however. He joined a caravan at Tunis and became a qadi for the people assembled to continue the trip. (The annual caravans of the *hajj* were so large that they required a formal government, usually an amir [chief] and a qadi.) While the caravan was in a town called Safaqis, Ibn Battutah enacted a marriage contract for the daughter of an official from Tunis. Soon after, though, he had a quarrel with his father-in-law and returned the woman. He then took another wife, the daughter of a man from Fez. He was so pleased with this marriage that he arranged a wedding feast that included all the caravan as guests; the celebration held up the caravan for a day.

▲ Cairo's Imam El Shafei cemetery; in Ibn Battutah's time this old Egyptian city was one of the largest in the world.

Although Ibn Battutah's own account seldom mentions his wife, it is known that he married several other women and took more women as slaves and concubines. Ibn Battutah indulged himself in another way as well —he seems to have divorced as easily as he married.

Travels in Egypt. Few travelers passed through Alexandria without hastening to add Cairo to their itinerary. At the time, the city had a population of five hundred thousand or more and was a great shopping center. Ibn Battutah took note of the sights of this great metropolis. He then decided to reach Mecca by traveling up the Nile River, proceeding overland to the Red Sea and across it to the Holy City. Unfortunately, shipping on the Red Sea had been interrupted and he was forced to return by land to Cairo and then head north to Damascus.

Damascus and Mecca. Ibn Battutah remained in Damascus for a month to study more about the law (he claimed to have completed fourteen courses in his month's stay). When he arrived at Mecca, he performed the rituals of Islam and took careful note to describe them and the holy city. Then he returned home. The entire trip, which he recorded faithfully, had taken him more than four thousand miles away from home and lasted for fourteen months.

Traveling the Nile River

It was not too difficult to return by way of Egypt for, as Ibn Battutah later wrote:

> There is no need for a traveler on the Nile to take any provision with him, because whenever he wishes to descend on the bank he may do so.... Cities and villages succeed one another along its bank without interruption and have no equal in the inhabited world. (Dunn, p. 43)

Later trips. By the late 1320s, Ibn Battutah was on the road again. This time he took a ship along the north coast of Africa, disembarked at Tanzania, and explored Iraq and Persia before again going to Mecca, reaching it by way of crossing Arabia from the Persian Gulf. He then explored the coast of Africa before sailing through the Red Sea into the Arabian Sea, along the coast of Arabia, and finally passing through the Gulf of Oman.

Two years later he traveled to India. Most North African visitors to India sailed across the Arabian Sea, but Ibn Battutah chose the long route. He traveled through Egypt and then north to Syria and Asia Minor, where he took a detour to explore Constantinople, next sailing the Black Sea to western Asia. At last he headed east across Afghanistan to reach the Indus River and Delhi. There his law studies earned him a position as judge in the court of Sultan Muhammad Tughluq. Ibn Battutah remained in India for eight

▲ A mosaic of life on the Nile River; Ibn Battutah wrote that "cities and villages succeed one another along its bank without interruption and have no equal in the inhabited world."

years. Once he was commissioned to lead an expedition to China, but that trip ended in a shipwreck that left him abandoned on the southwest coast of India. He took advantage of this disaster by visiting Ceylon and the Maldives, where he was again employed as a judge.

151

His expedition to China had failed, but Ibn Battutah was a determined traveler. In 1345 he decided to travel to China by himself. He sailed to the coast of Burma, then to the island of Sumatra, finally landing on the southern coast of China. A year later, he returned to Mecca by sea. Everywhere he went he took notes on the buildings, landscapes, religions, and people he encountered.

Excerpts From the *Rihla:*

"One day I had gone to the Nil [Nile] to accomplish a need when one of the Sudan came and stood between me and the river. I was amazed at his ill manners and lack of modesty and mentioned this to somebody, who said: `He did that only because he feared for you on account of the crocodile, so he placed himself between you and it.'" (Battutah in Dunn, p. 300)

Ibn Battutah's description of Taghaza, a town in the Sahara Desert: "An unattractive village, with the curious feature that its houses and mosques are built of blocks of salt, roofed with camel skins. There are no trees there, nothing but sand. In the sand is a salt mine; they dig for the salt, and find it in thick slabs." (Battutah in Chu and Skinner, p. 33)

Home. From Mecca, Ibn Battutah headed back to North Africa, reaching Fez, the capital of Morocco, before heading out again across the Strait of Gibraltar to visit the Islamic stronghold of Granada in Spain. Four years later, he embarked on another trip—this time by camel across the Sahara Desert to the kingdom of Mali in West Africa.

Aftermath

If Ibn Battutah had lived in the twentieth century his travels would have taken him to forty-four countries. He had been on the road for nearly thirty years and had covered about seventy-three thousand miles.

Upon hearing of his exploits, Sultan Abu Inan, ruler of Morocco, ordered Ibn Battutah to record his experiences and assigned a young literature student, Ibn Juzayy, to help him. The two were to write a book of travels, a *rihla*. The book immediately became controversial in Morocco—some scholars thought that the stories it contained were too fanciful to be true.

It was many years before other travelers began to confirm the accuracy of Ibn Battutah's geographic descriptions and the rihla began to be accepted. But Ibn Battutah still did not gain respect in his home country. He died in 1368 or 1369, without leaving a record of his last days. One ancient writer records only that he held the office of qadi somewhere. The importance of his travel accounts did not become clear to other scholars until the mid-nineteenth century.

Ibn Battutah's great work was translated into French and published in Paris in 1859. The entire account required four printed volumes.

For More Information

Chu, Daniel, and Elliott Skinner. *A Glorious Age in Africa.* Garden City, New York: Doubleday, 1965.

Dunn, Ross E. *The Adventures of Ibn Battuta, A Muslim Traveler of the 14th Century.* London: Croom Helm, 1986.

Gibb, H. A. R. *Ibn Battuta: Travels in Asia and Africa.* London: Routledge & Kegan Paul, 1929.

Trimingham, J. Spencer. *A History of Islam in West Africa.* Oxford, England: Oxford University Press, 1962.

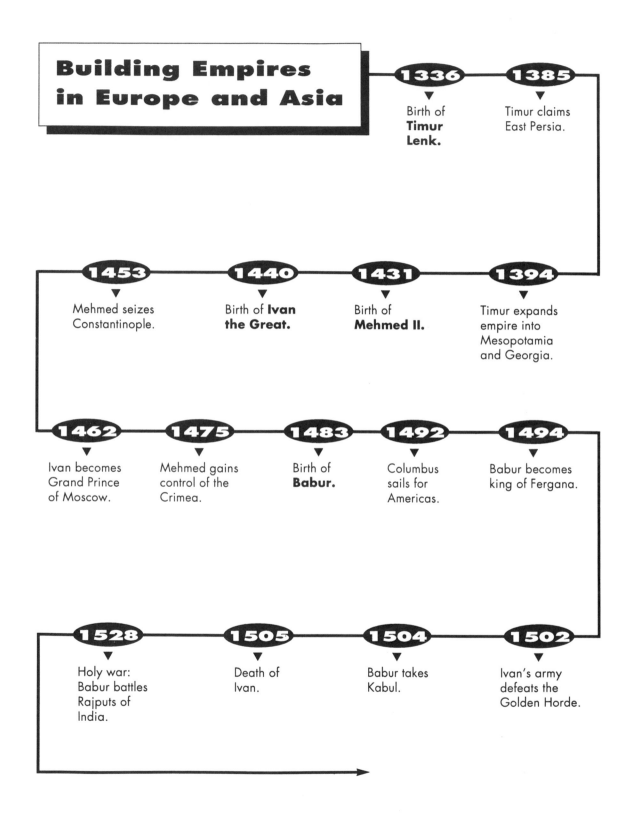

Building Empires in Europe and Asia

1336
▼
Birth of **Timur Lenk.**

1385
▼
Timur claims East Persia.

1453
▼
Mehmed seizes Constantinople.

1440
▼
Birth of **Ivan the Great.**

1431
▼
Birth of **Mehmed II.**

1394
▼
Timur expands empire into Mesopotamia and Georgia.

1462
▼
Ivan becomes Grand Prince of Moscow.

1475
▼
Mehmed gains control of the Crimea.

1483
▼
Birth of **Babur.**

1492
▼
Columbus sails for Americas.

1494
▼
Babur becomes king of Fergana.

1528
▼
Holy war: Babur battles Rajputs of India.

1505
▼
Death of Ivan.

1504
▼
Babur takes Kabul.

1502
▼
Ivan's army defeats the Golden Horde.

BUILDING EMPIRES IN EUROPE AND ASIA

About the same time that the Inca people were dominating one group after another to form an empire that stretched the length of South America, a small group of Asian tribes began expanding its control across Mongolia and into China. Perhaps one of the first global empires—one that spanned more than a single continent—was that of Genghis Khan. His thirteenth-century empire began in Mongolia and grew to encompass all of China and some of Korea. Genghis's military excursions took him across the Middle East into Russia and eastern Europe. The Great Khan himself broke up this global empire, dividing it among his sons.

Renewing the Mongol Empire. More than a hundred years later, **Timur Lenk,** descended from a people that had been conquered by Genghis in what is now Uzbekistan, set out to build a new global empire by recovering the lands of his ancestors. Beginning almost hopelessly—his mother died while he was young and his father abandoned him for life in a monastery—Timur learned the skills of warfare, built an army, and proceeded to cut down his opponents to the north and east. Eventually, he extended his authority from India to Russia and into eastern Europe. His Mongol Empire spread over nearly half the known world to include Turks, Persians, Indians, and Tatars, as well as Mongols. His army reached Delhi in India, where he is

▲ **The Great Wall of China; the Chinese built the Great Wall to keep the Mongols out of their country.**

said to have thoroughly looted the city and killed more than a hundred thousand of its citizens before turning home to Samarkand. Timur, who had become known as Timur Lenk (Timur the Lame) because of battle injuries, also built his capital at Samarkand, making it one of the era's great centers of art and literature.

The Ottoman Empire. But when Timur died, the great Mongol Empire once again disintegrated. It would remain fragmented for more than half a century, until another leader emerged to again revive the empire of Genghis Khan. The son of a sultan who was the ruler of the Turkish Ottoman Empire, **Mehmed II** took charge of an already enormous empire and expanded it, first by eliminating the vestiges of the long-lived Byzantine Empire and taking its capital, Constantinople, as his own, and then through excursions into Europe. Mehmed would live to see his global empire extend from Persia to Albania and from Russia to Egypt.

Russia. Far to the north and east, the grand prince of a principality called Muscovy set out to unite the many small states that are now part of Russia. Sending his diplomats and soldiers across the sometimes desolate land, the man who would become known as **Ivan the Great** succeeded in uniting land after land until he was ruler of a huge area of eastern Europe and northern Asia. In this way Ivan established the Russian Empire.

The Moghul Empire. Farther east, the subcontinent of India had shaken off the control of the Mongols and broken into small kingdoms. There, too, the leader of a small principality aspired to build a great nation. **Babur** forged the Muslim Moghul Empire, with headquarters at Agra, India. His military genius gave him control of an empire that stretched across the Middle East and into the Indian subcontinent.

These successful attempts to create multicontinental empires would have particular influence in Europe, foreshadowing the imperialism of rising European powers.

Timur Lenk

1336-1405

Personal Background

Lonely childhood. Timur Lenk (also known as Timur Leng and in English as Tamerlane or Tamburlaine) was born in Kesh, Transoxania (currently Uzbekistan in central Asia) in 1336. He was an only child and spent a very solitary youth. His mother died while he was young, and his father, Taragai, joined a monastery while Timur was still a boy. Timur's only companions during his childhood were his dogs and falcons. As a result of his years alone, he became a very serious and self-reliant person.

Nomadic spirit. A descendent of the Barlas clan of Turkic wanderers, Timur inherited his ancestors' nomadic temperament and zest for battle. The Barlas clan had fought with Chagatai—Genghis Khan's son, who governed the Mongol Empire after the death of his father. Thereafter, the clan scattered throughout the mountains of central Asia. Like most of the Barlas tribe, Timur preferred the open road to settlement and believed that only "a coward builds a [home] to hide in" (Lamb, p. 24).

Warrior education. Because of his wanderlust and desire to learn, Timur went to serve Kazgan the King-Maker when he turned seventeen. Amir (Arabic for "commander") Kazgan was the ruler of Transoxania and regularly accepted boys into his Tatar army, where they learned to fight. Though Kazgan did not always teach him directly, Timur learned a great deal through

▲ Timur Lenk

Event: Renewing the Mongol Empire.

Role: One of the last great conquerors to succeed by the sword, Timur Lenk re-established the Mongol Empire founded by Genghis Khan. In addition to extending the empire from India to the Mediterranean Sea, Timur brought about the "Timurid Renaissance," making his capital of Samarkand a world-renowned center of scholarship, art, architecture, commerce, and science.

▲ **Mongolian chiefs engaged in the royal sport of falconry; after he was abandoned by his father, Timur's only companions were his dogs and falcons.**

observation. He became a skilled horseman and swordfighter, learned to play chess and polo, and memorized the teachings of the Koran. From Kazgan he was taught that "brothers outweigh religion" (Lamb, p. 32). From this, Timur determined that his path would be forged as a leader of men and that he could accept all men—regardless of religion—into his service as long as they remained loyal "brothers."

Timur engaged in many battles for Kazgan and won the respect of the *bahaturs,* the most valiant warriors in the Tatar army. Timur became known as "a breeder of action ... in love with risk" and soon asked to be named head of the scattered Barlas clan, who were also known as the "helmeted men" of the mountains (Lamb, p. 35). Though impressed by Timur's ambition, Kazgan thought him still too young to lead such a large group. To subdue him for a while, Kazgan arranged for Timur to marry his granddaughter, Aljai Khatun Agha—the first of several wives he would have throughout his life.

Manhood and power. From age twenty to twenty-four, Timur lived with Aljai. However, as had become his custom, Timur spent very little time at home. He was made *ming-bashi,* or commander, of Kazgan's first infantry, in charge of a thousand men. As such, he engaged in battles throughout the western desert and southern valleys of Transoxania—all of which he won. During this time his first son, Jahangir, or "World Gripper," was born.

While Timur was away fighting, a revolt occurred within the Tatar ranks and Kazgan was killed. Fiercely loyal to his mentor, Timur tracked down the men responsible for his death and killed them. But Timur's action did not prevent a power struggle for control of Kazgan's kingdom from ensuing between two Tatar commanders, Hadji Barlas and Tughluq Temur. Too young and inexperienced to take power himself, Timur joined Tughluq, who became ruler in Kazgan's place. Tughluq appointed Timur *tuman-bashi,* or leader of ten thousand, and made him prince of the city of Samarkand. But after Kazgan's death, Timur was not content to follow anyone, and he soon rebelled against Tughluq. Because of his insubordination, a death warrant was issued by Tughluq, and Timur was forced to flee Samarkand with his family, becoming an outlaw.

> ## Tatars and Mongols
>
> The Tatars were nomads who lived east of the Mongols. In A.D. 1200 they were conquered by the Mongols, led by Genghis Khan, and became part of the Mongol Empire.
>
> The Mongols, meaning "brave people," descended from the Tungusi, a nomadic, aboriginal tribe of Turkish descent. Centered in Siberia, they were cousins of the Huns and Alans. The Chinese built the Great Wall to keep them out.

Participation: Restoring the Mongol Empire

Outlaw maimed. For the next few years, Timur lived in hiding in the desert with his family and a small band of followers. With his brother-in-law, Amir Hussayn, Timur organized an army and began leading attacks against Tughluq and several other warring regional factions—including the Jats, the Sijistanis, and the khans of Jatah—in an effort to take control of Samarkand and reunite the Tatar army under him. While fighting against the Sijistanis in what is now Afghanistan, Timur was wounded by arrows in the right hand and foot. Though he won the battle, he was maimed for life and was thereafter known as Timur Lenk, meaning "Timur the Lame."

Advances and setbacks. After winning battles from the Indian border to the Aral Sea, Hussayn and Timur succeeded in uniting the Tatars under their mutual rule. But dissension and death soon ripped apart their alliance. Timur's wife died in approximately 1360, his family tie to his brother-in-law thus severed. Timur turned against Hussayn. For the next decade, he and Hussayn engaged in a civil war that split the loyalties of the Tatars between the two leaders. But because of Timur's great skill as a leader and his reputation as a man of "unbending iron," most Tatar lords had come to his side by 1369 (Lamb, p. 77). Even some of his enemies, including the Jalairs, were so impressed by Timur's strength and determination that they too joined his cause. With the addition of the Jalairs, Timur's fighting force numbered in the hundreds of thousands. He easily defeated Hussayn and, upon his brother-in-law's defeat, was elected amir, or emperor, of the Tatars at age thirty-four. The Mongols, part of the Tatar army, swore their allegiance to Timur, and thus began the restoration of the Mongol Empire.

Always on the move. Though Timur could have easily been content to rule his lands from Samarkand, it was not in his nature. Instead of settling down he embarked on a mission to conquer all of central Asia and make the Mongol Empire one of the largest and most powerful in the world. He demonstrated his reach with attacks on the Golden Horde, who controlled much of Russia, eastern Europe, and China. For more than a decade, he fought the Horde with his formidable army and finally secured their defeat in 1397.

Never long off the battlefield, he invaded India the following year. His army marched on Delhi in December, leveling the city, and ousting its Hindu leaders. He replaced them with Muslims,

▲ **Mongol camp on the move; instead of settling down, Timur embarked on a mission to conquer all of central Asia and make the Mongol Empire one of the largest and most powerful in the world.**

which laid the foundation for the Moghul dynasty of Islamic rulers of India. His next conquest came less than a year later, when he attacked the Ottomans in the west. Led by Sultan Bayazid, the Ottomans had taken some of Timur's land while he was fighting in the east. To punish them, Timur re-captured Azerbaijan and ransacked most of what is now Syria, Iraq, and Iran, which the Ottomans had controlled. The Mongols then drove the Ottomans from eastern Europe, where they were preparing to invade western Europe and take Constantinople. By 1402 the Ottoman Empire was in shambles and Bayazid himself had been captured. In contrast, Timur's empire now stretched from India to the Mediterranean Sea. He controlled nearly half the known world.

The Timurid Renaissance. Timur established his capital at Samarkand and in 1399 began rebuilding the city in the model of other great cities he had seen during his travels throughout

India, the Middle East, eastern Europe, Russia, and Asia. He commissioned the construction of mosques, gardens, roads, colleges, libraries, a central plaza, an observatory, and the famed "white palace." He also recruited scholars, artists, and business leaders from throughout the world to teach and work in Samarkand. Though a soldier first and foremost, Timur appreciated art and architecture and cultivated a deep interest in history and science. Though illiterate, he was an avid student who often brought scholars with him—even in conquest—to read to him nightly. He is best known as the restorer of the Mongol Empire, but perhaps Timur's greatest contribution was the culture and commerce he inspired. His efforts became known as the "Timurid Renaissance," which lasted through 1506.

Timur and the Turks

On the threshold of Europe, Timur could have invaded the continent, but he chose not to. Like many Muslim rulers of the East, Timur had a general lack of respect for or interest in anything European. Nonetheless his defeat of the Ottoman Turks delayed by fifty years their conquest of Byzantium and permanently staved off an Ottoman invasion of western Europe. As a result, European leaders from Spain's King Henry III to Emperor Manuel of Constantinople paid tribute to Timur, whom they regarded with both gratitude and fear.

Brutal and clever. In battle, Timur lived by three rules: 1) Always fight on enemy soil, never at home; 2) Always attack first; and 3) Always attack as swiftly and as hard as hard-driven horses can travel. These tactics proved highly successful and enabled Timur to succeed even when he was outnumbered. He also believed in lavishly rewarding his soldiers and subjects for their loyalty to him. Among them he divided the spoils of victory—including gold, silver, and furs—and rarely kept anything for himself.

But while Timur was respected by his subjects, he was feared and loathed by his enemies. He was known by his opponents as a "bloody dog" bent on war, building pyramids from the skulls of defeated enemies (Lamb, p. 209). He also had a reputation for burning cities to the ground once he raided them, as he did in Baghdad and Delhi.

Timur could also be brutal to his own subjects. He did not tolerate any form of weakness or disloyalty and ruled his empire with an iron fist. He commonly killed beggars, handicapped persons, and thieves because he considered them weak.

Aftermath

One last conquest attempted. At sixty-nine years old and nearly blind, Timur set out on one last conquest. He wanted to add Cathay (China), then the richest empire in the world, to his Mongol Empire. In 1405 he led a force of two hundred thousand through the Gobi Desert. But before he could reach China, he fell ill and died, on January 19, 1405. The white charger he had been riding was sent on toward China out of respect and his body was taken back to Samarkand.

Before he died, Timur named a successor (one of his grandsons—all of his sons had died) and urged that the campaign in China continue without him. However, without his strong leadership, the army became disjointed and the invasion was abandoned. Soon a power struggle arose for control of the vast empire, and Timur's successor was beaten out by a challenger.

Legacy. As a military commander, Timur united Mongols, Turks, Persians, Afghans, and Syrians and made his army one of the most successful ever assembled. Together the Tatar/Mongol army fought over the course of three generations and conquered nearly half the

The Conquests of Timur Lenk	
1381	Herat, Persia
1383-85	Khorason and East Persia
1386-87	Armenia and Azerbaijan
1394	Mesopotamia and Georgia
1397	Russia (occupied Moscow)
1398	Northern India

known world. For this, Timur is remembered as the last great conqueror. For this also, many, including literary giant John Milton, considered him "the devil" (Hookham, p, 8). Whatever the label, Timur firmly re-established and greatly expand the Mongol Empire and laid the foundation of the Moghul Empire in India. He also brought about a cultural renaissance that lasted more than a century and has a continuing influence today.

For More Information

Hookham, Hilda. *Tamburlaine the Conqueror.* London: Hodder and Stoughton, 1962.

Lamb, Harold. *Tamerlane.* New York: Garden City, 1928.

Manz, Beatrice Forbes. *The Rise and Rule of Tamerlane.* Cambridge, England: Cambridge University Press, 1989.

Mehmed II

1432-1481

Personal Background

Son of a Sultan. Mehmed II, also known as Muhammad II, was born in 1432 into the family of Murad II, sultan of the Islamic Ottoman Empire. He was born during a time of great expansion for the empire. His father was the tenth in a line of Turkish sultans who had moved from their home in the north to dominate a large area the center of which is today Turkey. While Mehmed was a small boy, Murad was attempting to expand his realm east and west—west as far as Salonica (now northern Greece), Hungary, and Poland. At the same time, the wealthy sultan encouraged learning among the Turks. He is said to have supported Turkish poetry, law, and the study of Muslim theology. His sons, of which there were at least three, were educated in all of these subjects and also received the necessary training for war and government.

Mehmed was an excellent student. Besides developing a deep interest in Islam, he learned to speak five languages. He grew to share his father's interest in poetry. He also developed an almost uncontrollable temper. As Mehmed reached his twelfth birthday, his father's army was beaten in a battle for Belgrade (in Serbia). Murad had besieged the town but was defeated by a heroic general, Janos Hunyadi. In the course of the struggle, one of Murad's sons was killed.

Sultan of the Ottoman Empire. Perhaps depressed over

▲ **Mehmed II**

Event: The conquest of Constantinople.

Role: Mehmed II, sultan of the Ottoman Empire, besieged the declining Byzantine capital of Constantinople with an army estimated to have been stronger than seventy thousand soldiers. He then entered the city, making it an Islamic stronghold and the capital of his empire. The seizure of Constantinople paved the way for further Ottoman expansion, which reached as far as Bulgaria and even to part of Italy.

this turn of events, and feeling that he had his empire well in hand, Murad decided to give up his throne to his son Mehmed. The twelve-year-old boy took control of an empire that stretched from Hungary to beyond Persia and from Russia to Egypt. But the Hungarians rose up in rebellion, and the experienced Murad had to return to the throne after two years. Six years later, Mehmed took the throne as sultan again. He feared that other Ottoman men, including his brother, would challenge him as they had challenged his grandfather during his rule. He demonstrated his power in his first act as sultan: he ordered his own brother put to death. Next, he had an opportunity to practice his war skills while putting down a rebellion in one of his provinces, Karamania. That accomplished, Mehmed turned his attention to expanding the empire.

Remains of Byzantium. His own capital, Adrianople (now Edirne), in northwest Turkey, was the center of the vast empire built by his father and grandfather. Surrounded by the Ottoman Empire were the remains of the old Byzantine Empire. All that was left after crusaders destroyed it at the beginning of the thirteenth century was the aging capital, Constantinople. The city had dwindled in population as it endured twenty-eight sieges by the small nations that had broken away from the Byzantine Empire, and by Mehmed's time, it had fallen into decay. In the mid-fifteenth century the magnificent buildings of the city were supported by a population of about fifty thousand people. Even so, Constantinople was a key trading city and Mehmed planned to capture it. In 1453 his army set out for the city.

The defenses of Constantinople. It would not be an easy conquest even for an army of more than seventy thousand men and a navy of 320 ships. Constantinople sat on the Bosphorus, a narrow waterway between Europe and Asia. It was surrounded on three sides by the Sea of Marmara, the Bosphorus, and a branch of the Bosphorus called the Golden Horn. The inland side was protected by a great wall that reached from water to water. The ramparts of this wall were ordinarily manned by nine thousand seasoned soldiers under the leadership of a fearless emperor, Constantine XI, and his chief aide, the grand duke and grand admiral Notaras.

▲ A street scene in Constantinople; Mehmed's seizure of the city paved the way for further Ottoman expansion, which reached as far as Bulgaria and even to part of Italy.

Participation: The Conquest of Constantinople

A rebel within. Only a year before, the emperor at Constantinople had finally reached an agreement with the pope that reestablished the seat of Christianity at Rome after decades of quarreling over the issue by the leaders of Rome and Byzantium. (The Byzantine Empire was Christian, but it was controlled by the Greek Orthodox Church, not the pope at Rome. For centuries, Constantinople had been considered the eastern capital of Christianity. And though the Catholic and Greek Orthodox churches were bound by a common belief in the teachings of Jesus Christ, they were frequently at odds over cultural, political, and religious differences.) Rome and Byzantium seemed united in their fight against the Turks (Ottomans). There was someone, however, who hated the agreement with Rome. Grand duke Notaras despised

Rome and had openly said that he preferred Muslim (Ottoman) rule to Roman rule. He would make a major contribution to the fall of Constantinople by opting out of the battle for its defense.

The twenty-ninth siege. In April, the Ottoman Mehmed led his men to the great wall that protected Constantinople. Unable to break through, he laid siege to the city. It was the twenty-ninth time that the city had been besieged and the stubborn citizens knew how to fight under these conditions. The Ottomans made raids on the wall with no success, and the siege dragged on. For fifty-three days the citizens were shut inside the wall unable to bring in food. The situation for the already poor citizens grew worse and worse. Constantine grew increasingly worried. On May 28, he led a small band of soldiers out of the city on a foray for food. When the party returned, either by accident or plot, a gate was left open behind them. That was the opportunity Mehmed needed. Some of his men entered the gate and eliminated the guard. On the twenty-ninth of May, 1453, the Turkish horde stormed into the city.

Constantine XI. Inside, the rulers of Constantinople and their aides fought valiantly, led by the great Genoese general Gian Guistiniani. But when he was wounded, the whole Byzantine fighting force seemed to lose heart. Constantine tried to bolster their spirits by leading the battle himself. In the end, knowing he was doomed, he asked to be killed by a Christian, but he was cut down by the swords of Turks from in front of him and behind him. The slaughter of the Byzantine soldiers was accomplished in eight hours, and Mehmed entered the city through a gate called St. Romanus. The sultan ordered the body of Constantine beheaded and the head exhibited on a prominent pillar in the city.

Mehmed granted his soldiers permission to plunder the city. Women were raped, the citizenry was robbed and killed, houses were looted. Everything that was not in a public building was fair prey for the Turks. (Mehmed had reserved the public buildings for the government.) The pillage continued for four days. When at last it was over, not much remained of the once magnificent city.

The ire of Mehmed. In this conquest, Mehmed again demonstrated the violence of his temper. He had been known to grant freedom to a defeated town only to vent his rage later by killing all the residents. Now he ordered certain Christian church buildings torn down.

Shortly after he entered the city, Mehmed visited the grand duke Notaras. He scolded him for not defending the city (the great admiral had stayed home during the battle), then rewarded him for his betrayal. Soon afterward, the sultan invited Notaras to dinner and declared that he wanted the admiral's fourteen-year-old son for his services. Notaras protested, whereupon Mehmed ordered all of Notaras's five sons assembled and killed along with their father—all but the fourteen-year-old, whom he kept for his service. No one dared challenge the authority of the sultan.

Good deeds and bad. After his initial cruelties to the citizens of Constantinople, Mehmed turned to rebuilding what had once been the most magnificent city in Europe. The sultan renamed the city Istanbul. He was determined to restore it to its earlier position as a key trade center. The first step was to move his capital from Adrianople, 130 miles to the northwest, to Istanbul. He visited the palace of the Byzantine emperors, but this had been nearly destroyed in the many sieges and the few hours of raiding by his own soldiers. Upon seeing the destruction, the tyrant became saddened and was heard to recite an old Persian poem: "The spider has wove his web in the imperial palace, and the owl hath sung her watch-song on the towers of Afrasiab" (Kelly, p. 86).

Mehmed the builder. If Istanbul was to regain its glory, it had to have sufficient population to maintain trade and manufacturing. Mehmed solved that problem by forcing people from other parts of his empire to move to the city. While quarters were being readied for them, he began his program of construction. The old and decaying Hippodrome, once a great stadium, was condemned,

---

St. Sophia

The first building the conqueror Mehmed entered in Constantinople was St. Sophia, or the Hagia Sophia, a church that stood as a symbol of Christianity. It had been built by the emperor Justinian and was completed in A.D. 562. Ten thousand workmen had labored for thirty years, using materials gathered from throughout the Byzantine Empire. Built on a square 241 feet long on each side, it was capped by a dome that rose 175 feet. The interior of the building took the form of a Greek cross. At one time, it was said to contain sacred vessels worth $65 million. Mehmed had its murals plastered over and made St. Sophia into a mosque. It remained a Muslim mosque until 1935, when Kemal Ataturk, president of Turkey, ordered it changed into a museum.

and a nearby site was later used to build a bright new mosque, the Blue Mosque. Just outside the old city all and near the Golden Horn waterway, Mehmed built his private mosque, Eyüp. Also, two Christian churches, the Church of the Holy Apostles and a smaller adjacent chapel were torn down and replaced over an eight-year period by Fatih Camii, the Mosque of the Conqueror. Mehmed ordered a college to be built for boys, the Court of Eight Colleges. And he ordered the construction of his palace, Topkapi.

Establishing order. In spite of his tyranny, Mehmed was a wise ruler. He realized that he needed the former citizens of Constantinople to remain in the city, so he allowed them to keep their religions and some of their churches and temples. He allowed Christians and Jews to practice their faiths and live in the city, but they were forced to pay a much higher tax than the Muslims. Furthermore, the Christians were tightly controlled; Mehmed himself chose a new patriarch to lead them.

The new ruler established a secular code of laws based on Muslim law. These statutes helped achieve an orderliness not only in Istanbul but throughout the Ottoman Empire. Nonetheless, they bore witness to the villainy of Mehmed. In preparing them, he remembered the battles his grandfather had waged with his own brothers over who should rule, and the real or imagined threat posed by his own brother. Mehmed decreed that the oldest male member of the family of Ottoman rulers should be the heir to the throne. He then recommended that this heir kill the other males who might threaten his rule. The practice was adopted by the rulers who followed Mehmed and helped to keep the growing empire secure from civil war for centuries.

Fear of the Turks

The awe inspired by the fierce-looking Turks is evident in this description of the sultan Mehmed's party as they entered Constantinople:

> The sultan himself passed in triumph through the gate of St. Romanus. He was attended by his viziers, bashaws, and guards, each of whom was robust as Hercules, dextrous as Apollo, and equal in battle to any ten of the race of ordinary mortals. (Kelly, p. 85)

Aftermath

Further conquests. All that remained of the Byzantine Empire was now in the hands of Mehmed. As Istanbul was restored and order brought to it, the sultan began to absorb the small kingdoms nearby that had earlier broken free of Byzantium. He quickly subdued Trebezoid, Morea, and Servia. He soon controlled all the land from ancient Macedonia to Persia. Mehmed then turned his attention to Europe. Romania and Albania became subjects of his attacks but were not easily taken. They were defended by two of the world's greatest military leaders: Janos Hunyadi (who had defeated Mehmed's father in Serbia in 1444) and Skanderbeg (George Castriota). Shortly after Skanderbeg's death in 1568, Mehmed finally added Albania to his realm. He saw that Negropointe (a large island now part of Greece) and the Crimea were added to his empire in 1570 and 1575, respectively. Mehmed died at Adrianople on June 2, 1481.

The Ottomans would continue to rule the territory comprising the Ottoman Empire until they were deposed in 1922, after siding with the Germans in World War I. In its greatest expanse, Ottoman land extended from Russia to Egypt and from Macedonia and Albania to Persia.

For More Information

Hourani, Albert. *The Story of the Arab People.* Cambridge, Massachusetts: Belknap Press, 1993.

Kelly, Lawrence. *Istanbul, A Traveler's Companion.* New York: Atheneum, 1987.

Kritovoulos. *The History of Mehmet the Conqueror.* Translated by Charles T. Riggs. Westport, Connecticut: Greenwood, 1970.

Ivan the Great

1440-1505

Personal Background

Born into conflict. Ivan III Vasilyevich was born on January 22, 1440, in Moscow (capital of the Russian principality of Muscovy), to Grand Prince Vasily II of Muscovy and Maria Yaroslavna. At the time of Ivan's birth, his father was engaged in a bloody civil war with his uncle, Prince Yury of Zvenigorod and Galich, who was contesting Vasily's right to rule Muscovy. In 1446 Vasily was blinded by a cousin during the conflict, taken captive, and ousted from the throne. Ivan, just six years old, had to be smuggled into a monastery for protection. The following year, Vasily was restored to power, and Ivan returned home after being promised in marriage to the daughter of one of his father's captors, the grand prince of Tver.

Learns from father. Though totally blind, Vasily reigned for fifteen years after his restoration. Ivan, successor to the throne, was continually by his father's side and learned a great deal about war and government from him. From 1447 to 1462, Ivan joined his father in battle against his relatives, as well as the Tatars, and played a role in the final defeat of his cousin, Dimitri Shemyaka. When his father died in March 1462, Ivan was well prepared to take his place as grand prince of Muscovy.

Accession and feuds. Ivan had married Maria, the grand prince of Tver's daughter, at age twelve, and his first son, Ivan IV,

▲ **Ivan the Great**

Event: Building the Russian Empire.

Role: Grand Prince of Muscovy, Ivan the Great unified Russia and laid the foundation for a centralized government. He established Moscow as "the third Rome" and made it a formidable political force in the world. For this, he is known as the father of modern Russia.

was born six years later. Ivan was twenty-two when he succeeded his father. For ten years, Ivan's accession to the throne went unchallenged. During that time, his three brothers, Boris, Andrei, and Yury, more or less obeyed their father's final request to "respect and obey your older brother, Ivan, in my place" (Grey, p. 16). But after Yury died in 1472, a family feud broke out. Ivan had taken all the land left by Yury, and his remaining brothers felt cheated by his actions. They openly rebelled against him in 1480, and from then on, he was forced to fight his enemies without their help.

State of the union. When Ivan came to power, most of what we now know as Russia was not yet under his control. For that matter, the Ukraine and upper Oka River territory were controlled by Poland-Lithuania, and Novgorod, to the north, had also joined that power. Many of the central territories of the area—so important to trade—were independent, and the Golden Horde, the last vestige of Tatar power in Russian lands, controlled the lower Oka. Like his father, Ivan was determined to bring these territories under Moscow's control. He not only wanted the lands because he felt they were his birthright, according to tradition, but he also wanted them in the name of the Greek/Russian Orthodox Church. Catholicism was rapidly expanding throughout Russia and Europe, and Muscovy was the last stronghold of the Orthodox Christian Church.

Birth Prophesy

When Ivan the Great was born, an old Russian monk made a prophecy about his future deeds. He told his archbishop:

> Truly it is to-day that the Grand Prince [Vasily] triumphs; God has given him an heir; I behold this child making himself illustrious by glorious deeds. He will subdue princes and peoples. But woe to Novgorod! Novgorod will fall at his feet, and never rise up again. (Rambaud, p. 161)

Participation: Building the Russian Empire

Novgorod. In 1471 Ivan launched his first attack against the principality of Novgorod. He warned before his attack:

> Mend your ways towards me, my patrimony, and recognize us; keep my name of Grand Prince in strictness and in honor as of old; and send to me representatives to do homage and to make

▲ The earliest Russian cossacks were fifteenth-century peasant-soldiers who organized into companies.

settlement. I desire to keep you, my patrimony, in good favor, in the old conditions (Wren, p. 129).

But Novgorod refused Ivan's demand. The principality recognized the King of Poland as their ruler and accepted the Catholic faith as their state religion.

Holy war. Ivan called his attack on Novgorod a "holy war" and persecuted its leaders "for their conspiracy and crime in seeking to take to Latinism" (Catholicism; Wren, p. 130). Because the conflict was viewed as sacred, it stirred great passions among the Russian peoples, who eagerly joined Ivan's cause. Russian troops surrounded the capital of Novgorod, cut supply lines, and starved the region. By the end of the year, Novgorod was crippled, but the war continued for seven more years. In 1478 Novgorod's leaders were captured and transported to Moscow, where they were tortured and killed. Ivan proclaimed that the principality of Novgorod was officially dead and its lands now part of the grand principality of Muscovy. He sent thousands of Muscovites to Novgorod to occupy it, and by 1489 it was thoroughly under Ivan's control.

Master diplomat. Ivan's second campaign illustrates his gift for diplomacy. The independent central provinces of Ryazan, Tver, Rostov, Vereia, Iaroslavl, and Bielozersk were key to forming the Russian Empire. But rather than attack them with military force, Ivan devised a plan to acquire them through negotiation. First, Ivan shrewdly arranged a marriage between the Prince of Ryazan and his sister, Anna Vassilievna. In this way, the regions under the Prince of Ryazan's control became Ivan's through marriage. Next, he moved toward the other territories. Already fearful of Ivan's forces after the defeat of Novgorod, the princes of Tver, Vereia, Beilozersk, Rostov, and Iaroslavl were alarmed when they received word that Ivan would be paying them a visit. He was accompanied by his "grand master of artillery," and when the princes saw the pair coming, they immediately surrendered (Rambaud, p. 165). Ivan was able to gain hundreds of thousands of subjects to fortify his army and add to the national treasury without firing a shot.

The power of Sophia. Ivan's first wife died in 1467, and his only son died shortly thereafter. Since it was vital that Ivan have an heir, an exhaustive search for a wife ensued. Zoë Palaeologus, niece of the last emperor of Byzantium, was chosen to be his bride. A ward of Cardinal Bassarion in Rome but Christian Orthodox by faith, she was married to Ivan in the Kremlin (the fortified center of Moscow) in 1472. She changed her name to Sophia and, as easily, changed the face of Muscovy forever.

The third Rome. Sophia's impact on Ivan and Russia was tremendous. Through her lineage, she linked Ivan to the great emperors of Byzantium and to the Roman caesars. That made him successor to the Christian eastern empire. Moscow added the double-headed eagle of Byzantium to its seal and officially became the capital of Orthodox Christians or "the third Rome" (Constantinople, former capital of the Byzantine Empire, being the second; Wren, p. 139). Sophia brought with her an Italian and Byzantine refinement that powerfully affected the culture and commerce of Russia. The Greek and Italian scholars, artists, military experts, and architects that she attracted to Moscow changed the face of the city and greatly aided Ivan in his conquest of Russian territory.

Moscow and Greek Learning

In addition to the people Sophia brought with her from Rome, she brought Greek books. These ancient manuscripts—most from the Byzantine Empire—began the Library of the Patriarchs. Because of his exposure to the Renaissance of the West, Ivan began importing scholars and artists to Russia on a regular basis and opened up trade with Europe.

A greatly renowned, intelligent, and ambitious woman, Sophia made Russia famous in Europe and alerted Ivan to the importance of the West. Previously, little was known in the West of Moscow and even less of Ivan. After their marriage, Europeans began to recognize Russia as a formidable world power. For the first time, Ivan was exposed to the Renaissance ideas of Europe and the cultural and scientific progress being made there. He began to incorporate some of these Renaissance ideals into the life of Moscow by supporting the arts and bringing scholars and artists to Russia. He established trade ties with Europe and opened up diplomatic relations with nations of the West. Sophia's influence also brought about changes in court etiquette. A new regal palace was built for the royal couple, and formalities were strictly observed at the capital. Government bureaucracy became much more centralized around the new headquarters.

The Golden Horde. With north and central Russia consolidated, Ivan turned his attention to conquering the Golden Horde. The Horde possessed the last stronghold of Tatar power in Russia, and Ivan was anxious to eliminate it once and for all. He had been carefully encircling the land occupied by the Horde since 1472, and in 1478 he attacked. In 1480 the Horde turned the tables on Ivan, allying themselves with Poland and counterattacking Moscow. But by this time Ivan's forces were very strong, and his subjects were bent on "lifting ... the Tatar yoke" from their land (Wren, p. 135). The Russians easily defeated the Horde, led by Khan Ahmed, in Moscow. Though sporadic skirmishes continued for several years, the last of the Horde finally fell, and Russian unification was basically complete by 1502.

Aftermath

The Sudebnik. After Ivan succeeded in consolidating the Russian Empire, he commissioned a code of law, called the Sudebnik, in 1497. Among other things, the code unified law throughout Russian lands and centralized power in Moscow. Ivan, as prince, or tsar, had ultimate authority, but there were now uniform laws to govern both subjects and government. Among other provisions of the code, the crime of murder was made punishable by death; women and minors would be provided with a state-appointed "champion" or public defender if they needed one in court; and safeguards were enacted to prevent the bribing of judges and state officials.

Character. Though little is known of Ivan's private life, it is apparent from his activities that he was a skilled diplomat and military commander who made the most of his opportunities. It is also clear that he took great pains to introduce Western culture and technology to Russia. He was later called "Ivan the Great" because of his significant role in bringing Russia more in line with the advanced nations of Europe.

Death. Disappointment and controversy marked the last years of Ivan's life. A bitter dispute over who would succeed him and depression over not being able to conquer Lithuania left Ivan feeling empty and unloved by his subjects. He died in Moscow on October 27, 1505, at the age of sixty-five. He was succeeded by his son, Vasily. His passing went publicly unmourned, and it was decades before the title "the Great" was attached to his name.

For More Information

Backus, Oswald Prentiss. *Motives of West Russian Nobles* in Deserting Lithuania for Moscow. Lawrence, Kansas: University of Kansas Press, 1957.

Grey, Ian. *Ivan III and Unification of Russia.* London: English University Press, 1964.

Hughes, Lindsay. *New Perspectives on Muscovite History.* London: St. Martin's, 1993.

Rambaud, Alfred. *The History of Russia.* New York: John B. Auden, 1878.

Wren, Melvin C. *The Course of Russian History.* New York: Macmillan, 1968.

Babur

1483-1530

Personal Background

Royal birth. Zahiru'din Muhammad, who became known as Babur, was born on February 15, 1483, in Fergana, a small kingdom in the upper valley of the Syr-Darya (present-day Turkestan). His father, Umar Shaik Mirza, was the king of Fergana. Babur was the eldest of three boys and five girls and heir to his father's throne.

Babur learned to speak Persian and a Turkic dialect and seems to have had military training as a young boy. He was religious—raised a Muslim—and must have learned a great deal about diplomacy and politics from his father.

Inherited ambition. A descendent of both Genghis Khan and **Timur Lenk** (see entry), Babur inherited the ambition and drive of his famous relatives. Like them, he believed that "better than life with a bad name is death with a good one," and he aimed to make a lasting impression on the world (Babur, p. 559). At age twelve, he was presented with his first opportunity to make his mark. His father, "a ruler of high ambition and great pretension ... always bent on conquest," died suddenly when a building collapsed on him (Babur, p. 12). Babur became king of Fergana in June 1494.

Enemies abound. When Babur took the throne, he faced a difficult challenge: two enemies were preparing to invade Fergana

▲ Babur

Event: Founding the Moghul Empire.

Role: A descendent of Timur Lenk and Genghis Khan, Babur founded the Moghul dynasty of Muslim rulers in India. He was also a gifted writer and poet whose memoirs, *The Babur-Nama,* are widely held as one of the finest autobiographies ever written.

▲ **Babur leading his troops in battle; Babur's show of strength and fearlessness bolstered his army.**

from opposite directions. Under the advisement of his wise grandmother, Babur rallied his troops and met his enemies head-on. This show of strength and fearlessness bolstered his army and gave his soldiers and subjects confidence in his leadership abilities. Both his enemies fled, and Babur succeeded in saving his country from invasion.

Wise counsel. Babur relied heavily on the counsel of his mother, Qutluq-nigar Khanim, and grandmother, Aisan-daulat Begim. Qutluq-nigar was Babur's constant companion, even, as he later noted, "in most of my guerilla expeditions and throneless times" (Babur, p. 12). He credited Aisan-daulat with possessing superior judgment and wisdom, which she tried to pass along to her grandson. "Few amongst women will have been my grandmother's equals for judgment and counsel; she was very wise and far-sighted and most affairs of mine were carried through under her advice," he reported (Babur, p. 43).

Eye to Samarkand—twice. Babur was proud of his lineage and thought especially highly of his ancestor Timur Lenk. Because of his high estimation of Timur, Timur's capital of Samarkand held broad appeal. Babur desperately wanted to sit on Timur's ancient throne. He believed that "few towns in the whole habitable world are so pleasant as Samarkand," and he embarked on a military expedition to acquire it (Babur, p. 74).

In 1496 Babur invaded the old city but was defeated. The following year he repeated his efforts and was successful, though his success was short-lived.

Though he finally sat on the throne at Samarkand, Babur had to abandon his dream and return to Fergana, where his subjects were rioting in his absence. To his great dismay, he arrived too late. The town of Andijan had been taken by rebels by the time his army returned to Fergana. When he tried to return to Samarkand, that too had been taken. His army had held the city for just one hundred days. Within a short time, Babur's entire world had collapsed. At age fifteen, he was forced to flee his own land.

Fugitive. Babur left for the countryside and became a homeless wanderer. "It was very hard and vexing to me," he recalled in his memoirs. "Never since I had ruled, had I been cut off like this from my retainers and my country; never since I had known myself, had I known such annoyance and such hardship" (Babur, p. 90).

> ### Marriage Among the Moghuls
>
> It was customary for Muslim rulers to have many wives and several mistresses. Babur had a total of seven wives and two mistresses, who bore him five children who survived him.

For the next seven years, Babur was a fugitive, desperately trying to reorganize his army and recapture territory. In 1504 he won Kabul (in present-day Afghanistan). His army was strengthened, and for the following three years, he consolidated his power around the city. He felt it was "God's bounty and mercy" that allowed him to obtain a kingdom again and he gave thanks (Srivastava, p. 12). Babur adopted the name of padshah, or emperor, and with his newfound strength once again tried to take Samarkand. This time he was able to hold the city for eight months. When he was defeated in Timur's ancient capital for the third time in 1512, he finally abandoned his childhood dream of possessing his ancestral kingdom. He now looked to the East, where he would ulitmately make his mark upon the world.

Participation: Founding the Moghul Empire

Hindustan. By age twenty-nine, Babur was coming into his own as a leader. Both his mother and grandmother had passed away, and his first son, Humayun, had been born of his third wife, Mahim, in 1508. Although Babur had finally realized the futility of taking Samarkand, his goal of ruling where Timur had did not change. He learned that Timur had once conquered India and it became Babur's goal to do the same. "As these several countries had once been held by the Turks [Timur's people]," Babur said, "I pictured them as my own, and was resolved to get them into my hands, whether peacefully or by force" (Srivastava, p. 14).

"Divine Right" Legacy of Timur

All of Timur's descendants felt they had a "divine right" (ordained from God) to possess land in and rule his vast empire. After Timur's passing in 1405, the Mongol Empire was divided among relatives and others who vied for control. India was now back in the hands of Hindu leaders, and Babur naturally believed that Timur's India rightfully belonged to him.

Military strategy. From 1514 to 1519, Babur prepared his army to invade Hindustan in northern India. He acquired the services of two top "artillery-men," Ustad Ali and Mustafa, who helped him gather a huge supply of firearms and ammunition (Srivastava, p. 13). The use of artillery and possession of a mammoth weapons supply, as well as tactics Babur learned from warring with various enemies over the years, proved to be the keys to victory.

Babur had learned a great deal from his defeats. He learned the art of ambush from the Mongols and Afghans; he learned the use of *tulghuma,* a clever tactic of turning on an enemy's flanks, from the Uzbeks; and from the Turks he learned the importance of having an abundance of firearms and an armed cavalry. Babur integrated all of these lessons into his own battle strategy, and in 1522 he put it to the test, commencing the invasion of Hindustan.

Acquires the Punjab. After a series of small victories,

Babur's army conquered the northwestern Punjab region of India in 1524—their greatest gain to date. Babur entered into a treaty with another ruler, Alam Khan, that outlined a plan to split India between them: the Punjab going to Babur and the area around Delhi to Alam. The agreement gave legitimacy to Babur's claim to the Indian throne, and for the first time he was recognized as the rightful Moghul king of the Punjab (the term "Moghul" denotes an Indian Muslim).

In spite of the Babur-Alam agreement, Babur intended to take all of northern India. One enemy remained: Ibrahim Lodi, who held the capital of Delhi. With his son Humayun fighting by his side, Babur fought his chief enemy through 1526. The Battle of Panipat (in the Punjab), on April 21, 1526, proved to be the blow that rid Babur of Ibrahim. That day, Ibrahim was killed along with fifteen thousand men, and Babur's army moved on to occupy Delhi. Thus the Moghul dynasty was born.

Holy war. Throughout 1528 Babur engaged in a *jihad,* or holy war, with the Hindu Rajputs (a military and landowning people of the Rajasthan [now Rajputana] region of India) to establish the supremacy of his rule and the Muslim religion in India. The Battle of Khanua was the decisive event in that war. Babur's Moghuls drove the Rajputs north into what is today Afghanistan, and the holy war was effectively won. Victory in one last conflict, with the Afghanis, which ended in 1529, gave Babur control of all of India.

Babur established his palace at Agra and had terraced gardens, baths, and various buildings constructed. He maintained order in his empire by dividing the country among his most loyal and powerful Moghul commanders. He devised far-reaching plans to further develop India, construct mosques, and better the lives of his subjects, but he would not live to see them implemented.

Aftermath

Sacrifice? In mid-1530 Babur's son, Humayun, became gravely ill. Desperately, Babur summoned every doctor and spiritual adviser he could find, but no remedy seemed to work and

Humayun's condition worsened. Finally, one adviser suggested that Babur make a sacrifice of the most valuable thing in Humayun's possession. Babur responded: "I am the most valuable thing that Humayun possesses ... I shall make myself a sacrifice for him" (Srivastava, p. 31). He offered himself to God and then circled his son's bed three times. Six months later, on December 26, 1530, Babur died, and Humayun, fully recovered, inherited his father's throne.

Character. During his military campaigns, Babur kept a diary, which was later published as his memoirs. He also composed poems and invented a style of verse called Mubaiyan. He kept company with the great poets of his day and, like his role model Timur, surrounded himself with scholars and artists. He was a strongly religious man who wrote, "Were the sword of the world to leap forth, it would cut not a vein till God will" (Hasan, p. 189). Babur also firmly believed that people are very fallible and should continually reflect upon the consequences of their actions: "In conquest and in government, though many things may have an outside appearance of reason and justice, yet one-hundred-thousand reflections are right and necessary as to the bearings of each one of them" (Babur, p. 103).

Babur believed in strict discipline and was a fearless conqueror. He burnt cities to the ground and severely punished people for disloyalty (though he did not kill them as did Timur, but rather, imprisoned them). His motto as a conqueror was: "Him who submits not, strike, strip, crush, and force to obey" (Hasan, p. 186).

Legacy. Though Babur founded the Moghul dynasty, he did not live long enough to enact great change. His grandson, Akbar, was the ruler who truly established and furthered the Moghul Empire. But Babur laid the foundation that brought India stability, a new language and literature, closer trade ties to Asia, the Muslim faith, and vast cultural change.

For More Information

Babur, Zahiru'din Muhammad. *The Babur-Nama*. London: Luzac, 1921.

Hasan, Mohibbul. *Babur, Founder of the Moghul Empire in India.* New Delhi: Manohar, 1985.

Srivastava, Ashirbadi Lai. *The Mughul Empire.* Agra, India: Shiva Lal Agarwala, 1966.

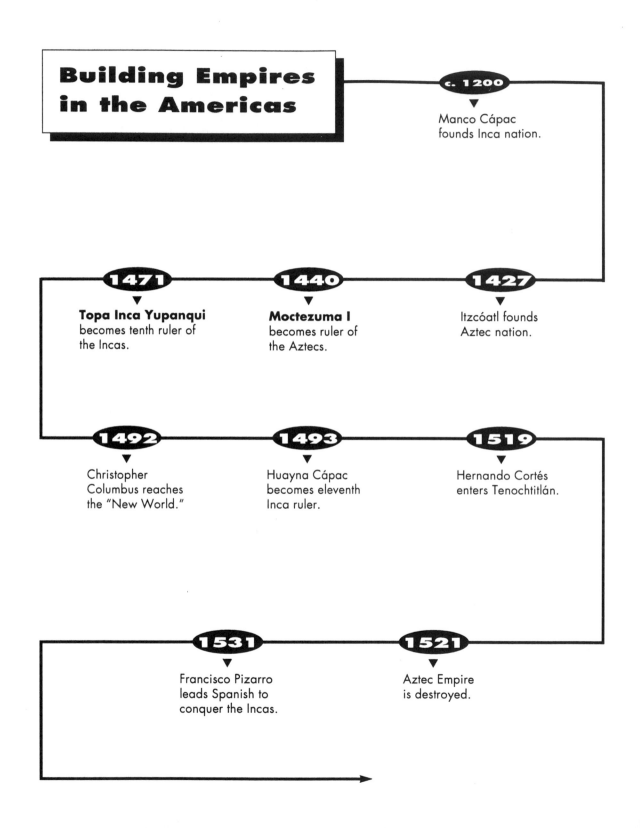

Building Empires in the Americas

c. 1200
Manco Cápac founds Inca nation.

1427
Itzcóatl founds Aztec nation.

1440
Moctezuma I becomes ruler of the Aztecs.

1471
Topa Inca Yupanqui becomes tenth ruler of the Incas.

1492
Christopher Columbus reaches the "New World."

1493
Huayna Cápac becomes eleventh Inca ruler.

1519
Hernando Cortés enters Tenochtitlán.

1521
Aztec Empire is destroyed.

1531
Francisco Pizarro leads Spanish to conquer the Incas.

BUILDING EMPIRES IN THE AMERICAS

The fifteenth century was a time of great political change. Until then, many lands that are now single countries were broken into small units over which monarchies (royal dynasties) presided.

Aztecs. On the land near what is now Mexico City, several tribes settled on a shallow lake or on an island in the lake. Each struggled to dominate those around them as they competed for food and clothing supplies during a period marked by drought. Gradually, most of the tribes were brought under the rule of an island people who called themselves the Mexica. These worshippers of a sun god built the Aztec Empire, organizing the various tribes into a tightly controlled economy based on corn and cotton. The Aztec Empire grew to the height of its power under **Moctezuma I.**

With labor demanded as tribute, Moctezuma and the Mexica made the great city of Tenochtitlán while the empire expanded north and east. As many as two hundred thousand lived in stone and thatch houses situated along the carefully laid out streets of the city. They established trade with many of the peoples around the lake—and conquered most of them. The residents of Tenochtitlán amassed great wealth in corn and gold. Their success and heavy-handed subjugation of conquered peo-

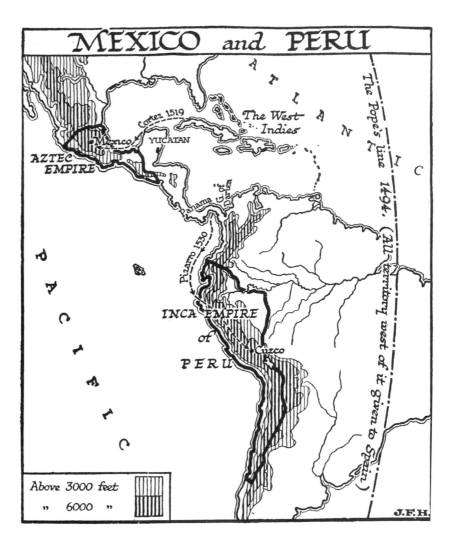

▲ **The Aztec Empire of Mexico and the Inca Empire of Peru.**

ples created many enemies. These foes were prepared to help anyone who promised to free them of the yoke of the Aztecs. In the sixteenth century, visiting Spaniards fulfilled that promise.

Incas. Two hundred years earlier, a small band of an agricultural people living in the Andes Mountains had set out, like the Aztecs, to ensure their food and clothing supply by conquering their neighbors. Unable to defeat the tribes east of them, who lived in the tropical forests, the Inca turned north and east from their base at Cuzco, in what is now Peru, and finally south to build an empire that reached from Quito in what is now Ecuador to the Maulé River in what we know as Chile.

The Inca were builders. Fine roads and great forts helped them control a highly diverse people. They amassed amazing wealth, most of which was stored in Cuzco. Under their tenth and eleventh leaders (**Topa Inca Yupanqui** and his son), the Inca Empire reached its zenith. A royal road 3,600 miles long linked all regions of the empire and aided the Incas in controlling the populace. But by the sixteenth century, the great empire had fallen into decline as ruling family members fought each other in a civil war. The empire's internal struggles, along with its well-established roads, made it easier for the Spanish to conquer the Incas and launch a "global" empire.

Topa Inca Yupanqui

c. 1445-1493

Personal Background

Son of an emperor. Topa Inca Yupanqui (or Tupac Yupanqui) was the youngest of several sons of Pachacútec, the ninth Inca ruler. His father had become king of a small agricultural community around the farming village of Cuzco in what is now Peru. A tall, inspiring man, Pachacútec had gathered soldiers and set out to organize the people who lived in the region. As the number of followers grew, he oversaw the construction of a great temple and built stone houses for Cuzco's growing population.

Wherever the armies went, roads were built of stone and walled on each side to prevent sliding in the steep mountains. Twenty-four feet in width, the roads made travel for war or trade easier. Great stone forts were built at regular intervals to suppress the rebellious tribes brought into Pachacútec's empire. These tribes grew in number almost constantly.

Yupanqui was born at Cuzco in about 1445. (The exact day and year is not known, though it is certain that Yupanqui was about fifteen years old when his father assigned him to his first army duty in 1160.) At the time of Yupanqui's birth, Cuzco was becoming a large and beautiful city. It had been founded by the first Inca, Manco Cápac, in about 1200. Cuzco had been built up around a great square, next to which were the Temple of the Sun and a House of the Sun Virgins, for the Incas worshipped a sun god.

▲ A carved Incan wooden vase; the Incas amassed great wealth, most of which was stored in their warehouses in the capital city of Cuzco.

Event: Expanding the Inca Empire.

Role: In an unusual event for the Incas, Topa Inca Yupanqui inherited the empire when his father, Pachacútec, abdicated the throne in his favor. Pachacútec, Yupanqui, and Yupanqui's son, Huayna Cápac, each had a hand in expanding the empire to its greatest power. At its height, the Inca Empire of South America stretched from Quito in present-day Ecuador to the Maulé River in Chile.

Inca Rulers

Following is a list of the Inca rulers. Historians have not established the exact dates of the reigns from Sinchi Roca to Virachocha Inca.

1. Manco Cápac founded the Inca society about A.D. 1200.

2. Sinchi Roca

3. Lloque Yupanqui

4. Mayta Cápac

5. Cápac Yupanqui

6. Inca Roca

7. Yahuar Huacac

8. Virachocha Inca

9. Pachacútec (1438-1471)

10. Topa Inca Yupanqui (1471-1493)

11. Huayna Cápac (1493-1525)

12. Huáscar (1525-1532) ruled in the south of a divided empire

13. Atahullpa (1532-1533)

(adapted from McKown 1966, p. 213)

Yupanqui's father had added to the population of Cuzco by bringing defeated enemies to settle there, where they could be taught the ways of the Incas and learn their language, Quechua. When Yupanqui was a child, about two hundred thousand people lived in Cuzco in steeply gabled, stone houses richly painted in reds, yellows, and blacks.

Early life. Not much is known about Yupanqui's childhood, except that his father had founded a boy's school in Cuzco for the sons of aristocrats, either those of Cuzco or of defeated rulers. Most likely Yupanqui attended this school to learn the ways of the "Incas," the name for the ruling class of kings and nobles. He was also probably taught to use the tools of war—bolas (a cord with weights [stones] attached to the ends that is thrown at and entangles an enemy), heavy fiber slings for throwing rocks, clubs, axes, and wooden spears tipped with metal. It is also almost certain that Yupanqui learned how to use the *quipu,* a rope from which hung a number of knotted strings. The accountants of Cuzco used the quipu to keep track of goods coming in from the expanding empire.

Undoubtedly the young Yupanqui had opportunities to watch his father's handling of defeated warriors. Parades of these ex-enemies entered Cuczo from time to time, to be led to the square, where the marchers were made to lie down, and then slowly walked upon by the victorious forces. Those who seemed to be particularly threatening to the Inca government were disposed of—sometimes in brutal fashion. But most prisoners were released to go home; some were even allowed to keep their government posts.

▲ Incan warriors, from an ancient Peruvian painting; Incas became well known and feared for acts that were sometimes extremely violent.

To war. Whatever Yupanqui's training and experience, by the time he was fifteen his father had sent him off to battle. He was to be guided by the best generals and learn military strategy from them. It was an odd arrangement; while learning from the generals, Yupanqui was also in charge of them as the emperor's son. His first adventures were to the north, where the Inca armies carried battle to tribes as far away as five hundred miles. Following his father's directions, Yupanqui first sent messengers to the potential foes, inviting them to surrender. Many did; others fought to the end. The Huanca people, for example, surrendered immediately and even brought Yupanqui treasures. But the jungle kingdom of the Chachas proved too strong, and Yupanqui had to abandon his efforts to conquer them.

Yupanqui then marched north to battle the Incas' arch enemies, the Cusibamba, and then south to the region of Lake Titicaca. Here he had more success. Everywhere his armies were victorious, or the people gave up without a battle. Yupanqui tried to secure the peaceful surrender of as many tribes as possible. But one city that had fought stubbornly was punished by having its men and pregnant women killed. The town was then destroyed.

As Yupanqui and his forces moved along, he expanded the royal road into newly conquered territories and erected forts and

▲ An Inca warrior with his club and shield, wearing a headdress emblazoned with a feline head.

new cities. Some became regional capitals. In these he built great plazas like the one in Cuzco, made of large stones so tightly fitted that they needed no cement—not even the blade of a knife could fit them. Yupanqui had a grand palace built at Ayaviri in 1450 and shortly afterward started building a road south to Lake Titicaca and onward into what is now Chile. Yupanqui held no slaves, as did rulers in other countries. All this grand construction was done by demanding government service (corveé labor) in each region he controlled.

Participation: Expanding the Inca Empire

Topa Inca. About 1471 Pachacútec decided that his son was worthy to rule all the Inca people. He, himself, had not fought a battle for ten years. Instead he had devoted his attention to building Cuzco into the most impressive city in the Americas, rich with the tributes demanded from conquered peoples. Gold and silver flowed into the city, and some of the buildings were plated with gold. Pachacútec abdicated his throne, giving control of the Inca and their subjects to Yupanqui, who became the tenth leader of the Incas. Three more rulers would follow him before the empire was destroyed by the Spanish, who, it is said, damaged more structures in the capital city in four years than the Incas had built in four hundred.

Topa Inca (the title means "only Inca") Yupanqui ruled as his father had. Each conquered state had its own governors. They were required to make sure corveé labor was completed and taxes were paid, which meant that all work in the empire was carefully controlled. To make sure that the governors, who were often the rulers of former enemies, minded Inca rule, clusters of Incas were moved to the regional capitals. These "mitimares" spied on the local government and made sure that correct taxes were collected and that the subjects put no other god above the sun god of the Incas. And the great roads that ran more than three thousand miles along the shore and mountains of South America, with toll posts and guard stations, ensured a close watch on all the subjects.

Marriage. In 1471, perhaps as part of the ceremony of induction as emperor, Topa Inca Yupanqui took a wife. Adhering to Inca tradition, he married his sister, Ocllo, thus ensuring the purity of the lineage. After the wedding, Ocllo was called Mama Ocllo.

Emperor Yupanaqui faced many challenges within his capital. The priests were a constant threat to his power. Revered because the Inca were a deeply religious people, and possessing the right to determine the most favorable time for events—the start of a march or battle, the beginning of a building project, the date of a festival, the hour of a sacrifice—the priests sometimes seemed poised to take over the government. Yupanqui thought them foolish and claimed they were only "petty magicians." One time Yupanqui grew so irritated at the priests that he ordered a bloodbath of those he dared to touch—the lower ranks of the priesthood. Although she had just given birth to a son and heir to the throne, Huayna Cápac, the compassionate Ocllo took up the cause of the priests and succeeded in saving them. After that she became the mediator between the emperor and the priests.

Inca Forts

Topa Inca Yupanqui had great forts built throughout his realm. These forts were designed to house the population of entire cities should the occasion arise. Sacsahuamán, situated north of Cuzco, was a three-story stone fort eighteen hundred feet long. It took twenty thousand corveé workers a period of more than ninety years to complete. The forts were needed because the conquered peoples sometimes rose up in rebellion against the Incas.

The limits of Inca land. Yupanqui continued to expand his empire, attacking the tribes that inhabited the far side of the Andes Mountains. But these were elusive foes, and he was never able to accomplish much on his eastern front. He had better success along the coast to the north and south. His armies marched into what is now Ecuador in the north, finding stubborn resistance from the people of Quito—it remained for his son to conquer this city. In the south, Yupanqui decided to take the entire coastal region that is now Chile. An army of thirty thousand men entered Chile with little trouble. Most of the people along the way simply gave up when they saw such a large and powerful force coming toward them. There was, however, one society powerful enough to resist the Incas, the Araucans. This large group based in central Chile put up such stout resistance that Yupanqui at last stopped his army. The southern end of the Inca Empire was fixed at the Maulé River.

In 1493 Yupanqui died. His oldest son, Huayna Cápac, was named to succeed him. He was still in his teens—not of age to take the throne—so Mama Ocllo helped her son through the first years. With her strong guidance, Huayna Cápac continued his father's plans for expansion. Additions to the royal highway extended it to 3,600 miles, from Quito to the Maulé River.

Huayna Cápac's army had finally defeated the well-organized and advanced kingdom of Quito, and thus the Inca Empire reached its apex. One year before Huayna Cápac's death, Spaniard Francisco Pizzaro landed on the coast of Columbia and began his exploration of South America. Then Huayna Cápac's death threw the Inca Empire into civil war. His two sons, Huáscar and Atahualpa, fought for control of the empire. By the time Atahualpa succeeded in killing his brother, the empire was already weak—so weak that he could not protect it from the few well-armed Spaniards who came seeking conquest. By 1533 the Inca Empire had disintegrated.

Birthplace of Huayna Cápac

Yupanqui and Ocllo's son was born in a new city, Tumpipampa (now Cuenca). The grandeur of the Incas is clear from a 1547 description of this city by the Spaniard Pedro de Cieza:

> The Temple of the Sun was stone built and set together without mortar and with the most subtle skill. The façades of the buildings were beautiful and highly decorated, some of them set with precious stones. The walls of the temple and the palaces of the Incas were covered with sheets of the finest gold. The roofs of these buildings are of a grass thatch so well laid that, barring a fire, it should last for ages. (Von Hagen, pp. 28-29)

For More Information

Engl, Lieselotte, and Theo Engl. *Twilight of Ancient Peru: The Glory and Decline of the Inca Empire.* Translated by Alisa Jaffe. New York: McGraw-Hill, 1969.

McKown, Robin. *The Story of the Incas: Mightiest Empire of the Early Americas.* New York: Putnam's Sons, 1966.

Métraux, Alfred. *The History of the Incas.* Translated by George Ordish. New York: Pantheon Books, 1969.

Von Hagen, Victor Wolfgang. *Royal Road of the Inca.* London: Gordon & Cremonesi, 1976.

Moctezuma I

1398-1469

Personal Background

Early life. Moctezuma was born into royalty in the year the Mexica (Aztecs) called Ten Rabbit, which today's Western calendar sets as 1398. Though the exact details of his childhood aren't known, some things can be assumed. The young Moctezuma, like other Mexica children, might have run barefoot along the paths of his village, Tenochtitlán. (Tenochtitlán is the ancient name of Mexico City. It would become the capital of the Aztec Empire.) He probably added to the family food supply by fishing with spears and nets in the channels around the area (Tenochtitlán was an island city).

Moctezuma certainly practiced warfare as well, even in peacetime, learning to shoot accurately with bow and arrow and to wage hand-to-hand fighting with knives made of flint. Such skills were important in this land where war was both a serious activity and a game. The people of Tenochtitlán worshipped a god who demanded human sacrifice. Victims were most often prisoners taken in raids on other towns. In addition, skirmishes between the people of Tenochtitlán and other towns on Lake Texcoco were common. Once, when Moctezuma was five, his townsmen wrecked the canoes of three other towns on the lake. And when he was nine, the people of Tenochtitlán accused a village across the lake, which handled the storage and shipping of corn, of dis-

▲ Aztec relics; under Moctezuma I the Aztec
Empire spread across Mexico from the
Gulf of Mexico to the Pacific Ocean.

Event: Building the Aztec Empire.

Role: The town of Tenochtitlán was but
one of several small kingdoms near Lake
Texcoco when Moctezuma led his warriors in battle against the other kingdoms.
One by one, they acknowledged the
authority of the people who called themselves Mexica but who are known today
as the Aztecs.

honesty. War would have certainly been the outcome if Itzcóatl, the king's half brother, had not negotiated the opening of trade routes to other locales on the lake. Nevertheless, the citizens of Tenochtitlán were well accustomed to fighting, and they believed, as prophesied in the vision of their city god, Huitzilopochtli, that they would some day rule the entire region.

Discord around the lake. Meanwhile, the ruler of another city, Azcapotzalco, was growing stronger—demanding allegiance and tribute from more and more of the cities in the area. But as Azcapotzalco's power broadened, so did that of Tenochtitlán. As Moctezuma grew to young manhood, the citizens of Tenochtitlán bargained for jade, turquoise, and gold in other cities and turned these raw products into beautiful jewelry. They fished the channels around the city and traded their catch in places that produced grain and cotton. The city prospered, and residents' old thatched huts were replaced by houses of stone. While Tenochtitlán grew more equal in wealth and power to Azcapotzalco, which demanded tribute from and granted water rights to Moctezuma's people, Azcapotzalco's ruler was losing his authority to Maxtla, a man who had his sights on capturing Tenochtitlán. When Moctezuma was twenty years old, war erupted between his city and those controlled by Azcapotzalco.

Before the Aztecs

Itzcóatl was not the first king of Tenochtitlán, but he was the first to expand the territory sufficiently to be called emperor of the Aztecs. Neither were the Mexicas the first to organize a great kingdom. Before A.D. 900 the region supported the kingdoms of the Toltecs, Anahuacans, Zapotecs, the Mixtecs, and others. All were powerful kingdoms, and some outlasted the Aztecs.

Itzcóatl. The people of Tenochtitlán needed a new ruler, one who could protect them in war and direct them in establishing a far-reaching empire. Itzcóatl, already the king of another island city, and Moctezuma, known for his skill as an archer, were the two contenders finally considered by the Mexica council. It looked as if the city would be divided over the selection, but Moctezuma resolved the issue. He was not yet thirty years old when he declared that Itzcóatl should be the ruler, and that he would assist as director of food and construction. That position gave him great authority over war, since war was a means of obtaining food.

Drought. No sooner had Itzcóatl become ruler than a severe drought began. Without rain, farmland dried up and corn withered on the stalk. Hunger and starvation plagued the people. Moctezuma persuaded Itzcóatl to allow the citizens to go to other places to live if they chose. Meanwhile, the director of food made plans to expand the nation and protect its food supply by capturing cities in the richer farmlands. But first, he had to secure Tenochtitlán against its old enemy, Azcapotzalco. Moctezuma was crossing the lake to plot with an old friend, the ruler of another city, when he was taken prisoner by an ally of Azcapotzalco, the city-kingdom of Chalco, led by Maxtla. Itzcóatl was not strong enough to rescue him—he even sent word that whatever the people of Chalco decided to do with the prisoners was acceptable to the people of Tenochtitlán. Moctezuma was scheduled to be killed.

But it was not to be. Moctezuma escaped, killing a man and his wife in a canoe, and paddled toward home. Shortly thereafter, the people of Tenochtitlán prepared for war with Maxtla and his city. It was the beginning of years of struggle.

Participation: Building the Aztec Empire

Building an empire. Now Tenochtitlán gathered its allies and built strong armies. Acting as the right hand of Itzcóatl, Moctezuma directed wars against the other island and coastal cities. The first victims to fall were the people of Azcapotzalco.

As Itzcóatl and Moctezuma defeated or accepted submission from one after another of the cities of the Lake Texcoco—Tlatelolco, Huixachtlan, Xochimilco, Cuchuacan, Cuitlahuac, and Chalco—Moctezuma gathered experts to help strengthen Tenochtitlán. A defeated city known for its engineering was called upon to build an aqueduct from the mountains to the city in order to bring a constant supply of fresh water to Tenochtitlán. Other cities sent builders to transform the city into one of stone buildings and to raise the altar to the city god, Huitzilopochtli, higher and higher. In a time of flood, workers were summoned to construct a barrier across the lake to protect Tenochtitlán from the mountain runoff.

Prisoners were led to Tenochtitlán to be fattened until they were suitable for sacrifice to the god of the city. They would then make the slow trek up the high stairs to the altar on which they would be sacrificed by having their hearts cut out and their blood poured over the other objects to be sacrificed.

For the Aztecs, war was highly ritualized. A prospective foe might be sent gifts that were unacceptable—insulting in their value or in meaning. If the receiver of the gift refused to accept it, war had been declared. The fighting continued until one side accepted total defeat and agreed to pay tribute to the other and do whatever was required of it. Often a victory was celebrated by forcing the opposing army to dance in its own city square in women's clothing. And usually defeat meant sending women to the victor's city as slaves, prostitutes, or potential sacrifices.

The death of Itzcóatl. In the year the Mexicas called Thirteen Stone (c. 1439), Itzcóatl died. After the traditional eighty days of mourning, the people began the process of selecting a new king. The city council appointed a small committee to make the decision, which would be approved by the rulers of Tenochtitlán's two allies, Texcoco and Tlacopan.

The committee narrowed the list of candidates to four and then to two: Moctezuma and his brother Tlacaelel. Both were well known among the allies and their enemies. Both had distinguished themselves in battle and both had been advisers to Itzcóatl. Moctezuma was out of town, so the committee first approached Tlacaelel. But Tlacaelel refused the position. "Better to be a councilor than to be a king," he said (Gillmor, p. 88).

Moctezuma was actually better known away from home than in Tenochtitlán. He had spent time in Texcoco, Chalco, Tlaxcala, and Huexotzinco building Mexica trade so that there was a rich supply of food and cotton coming into the city. And his mother was a foreigner from Cuauhnauac, a distant city, and Moctezuma had taken a wife from there. Then, too, the frowning countenance of the man called the Angry One, the Archer of the Skies, worked against his selection. In the end, however, his bravery and skill at war won him the committee's vote and the approval of the allies. Messengers were sent to see if Moctezuma would accept the election, and he was persuaded. On the day known as One Crocodile in the year 1440, Moctezuma became king of the Mexicas, inaugurated with proper ceremony, prayers, and sacrifices. A new council was also approved. It included his two sons, Citlalcohuatzin and Iquehuacatzin. Tlacaelel would be a high priest and chief adviser to the king.

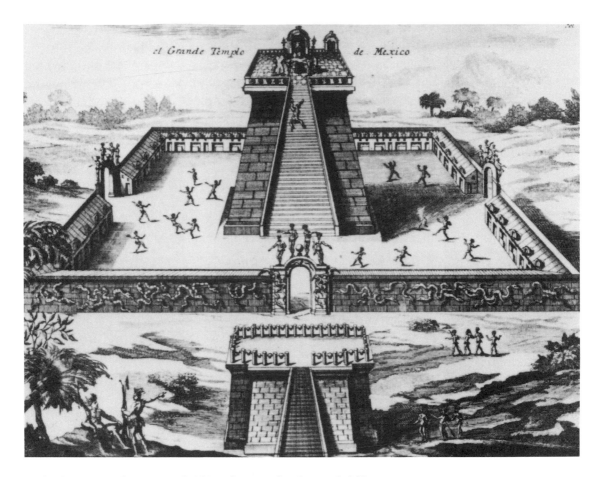

el Grande Templo de Mexico

▲ The huge temple at Tenochtitlán; the people of Tenochtitlán worshipped a god who demanded human sacrifice. Victims were most often prisoners taken in raids on other towns.

Expanding the realm. Almost as co-rulers, Moctezuma and Tlacaelel worked together to expand the rule of Mexica and establish an Aztec Empire that spread across today's Mexico from the Gulf of Mexico to the Pacific Ocean. Ambassadors were sent to every conquered city; they served to guide the government there and to collect the tribute demanded by Moctezuma. Tenochtitlán grew rich, with beautiful buildings and great stores of corn and gold. Nor did Moctezuma stop at Tenochtitlán. Grand temples were built in many of the vanquished cities, and roadways were improved to connect the important places in the empire.

Conditions of Peace

Tributes required by the Aztecs' from their enemies were designed to bring necessary products to Tenochtitlán. Following is part of the tribute claimed from the people of Tonotacs:

Twice a year	**Once a year**
400 women's blouses and skirts	2 warrior costumes
400 small cloaks	1 necklace of gems
400 half-quilted cloaks	2 crystal lip plugs
400 large cloaks	28 gold lip plugs
160 very rich robes for lords	400 lbs. of cocoa beans
1200 black and white striped cloaks	

Only two great issues still faced the new king: drought and the old enemy, Chalco. Almost immediately after he took office, a drought that lasted for six years struck the region. In his days as adviser to Itzcóatl, however, Moctezuma had established controls on trade far beyond the island, and tribute coming into the city allowed it to survive. Also vexing, the people of Chalco frequently rose up in rebellion. Moctezuma was forced time and time again to send troops to reestablish control. Finally, Chalco was beaten into complete submission. What had happened at Chalco would be replayed again and again, for as Moctezuma and his successors conquered one state and then another, imposing taxes and collecting tributes, the ruler of the Aztecs earned many enemies.

Aftermath

Culture. Once the Aztec Empire had been secured militarily, Moctezuma could turn his attention to cultural matters. He had, for example, long been impressed by the variety of vegetation in the empire, which now encompassed sea coasts, swamps, plains, and mountains. Moctezuma directed that plants from every region be gathered for a great botanical garden in Tenochtitlán.

Death. Moctezuma ruled over an ever-growing empire until he died at the age of seventy. His brother presided over the

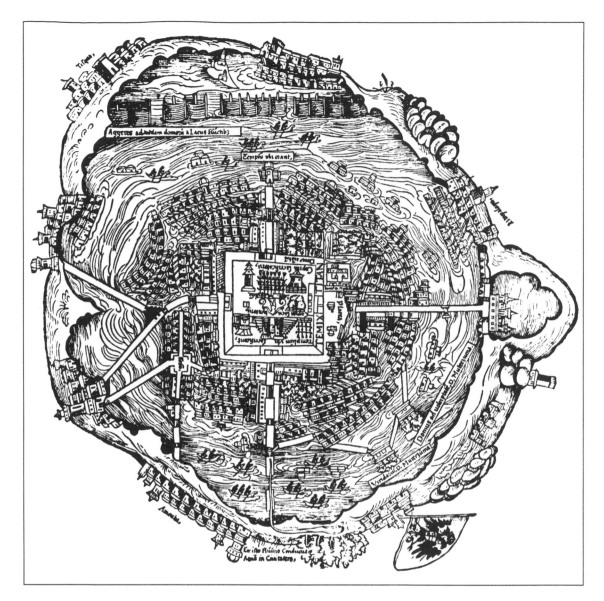

▲ The earliest-known sketch of Tenochtitlán, circa 1520; under
Moctezuma the city grew rich, with beautiful buildings and great
stores of corn and gold.

funeral and the mourning. Rulers of the neighboring towns sent
jewels to be buried with the body and slaves to be sacrificed.
Moctezuma's body was doubled knees to chest as was the custom, wrapped in clothing for the grave, and buried in the court-
yard of his home in Tenochtitlán.

Fall of the Aztecs. Less than fifty years after his death, strange visitors came to Tenochtitlán, then ruled by Moctezuma's great grandson, Moctezuma II, or Montezuma Xocoyotzin. The city was ill-prepared for the invasion of this small band of Spanish adventurers led by Hernando Cortés. Montezuma II's arrogance and favoritism for a few old nobles had made him unpopular. When it became necessary to defend the capital city, the old and festering ill feelings of the neighboring cities flared, and he found little support. Thus the vast Aztec Empire fell to a handful of Spanish soldiers in 1521.

For More Information

Gillmor, Francis. *The King Danced in the Marketplace.* Tucson: University of Arizona Press, 1964.

Ruiz, Ramón Eduardo. *Triumphs and Tragedy: A History of the Mexican People.* New York: W. W. Norton, 1992.

Thomas, Hugh. *Conquest: Montezuma, Cortes, and the Fall of Old Mexico.* New York: Simon and Schuster, 1994.

Bibliography

Babinger, Franz. *Mehmed the Conqueror and His Time.* Translated by Ralph Manheim. Princeton, New Jersey: Princeton University Press, 1978.

Baynes, Norman H. *The Byzantine Empire.* London: Oxford University Press, 1958.

Bohannan, Paul. *Africa and Africans.* Garden City, New York: Doubleday, 1964.

Charlesworth, M. P. *Trade-Routes and Commerce of the Roman Empire.* New York: Cambridge University Press, 1926.

Clari, Robert de. *The Conquest of Constantinople.* Translated by E. H. McNeal. New York: New York University Press, 1936.

Collier, George, editor. *Inca and Aztec States: Fourteen Hundred to Eighteen Hundred: Anthropology and History.* New York: Academic Press, 1982.

Davidson, Basil. *A History of West Africa to the Nineteenth Century.* Garden City, New York: Anchor Books, 1966.

Davidson, Basil. *The African Past.* Boston: Little, Brown, 1959.

Davies, Nigel. *The Ancient Kingdoms of Mexico.* New York: Viking-Penguin, 1982.

Diehl, Charles. *History of the Byzantine Empire.* New York: AMS, 1969.

Ellis, Edward S., and Charles F. Horne. *The World Famous Events.* New York: Francis R. Niglutsch, 1914.

Fage, J. D. *A History of Africa.* New York: Alfred A. Knopf, 1978.

Gibb, A. R. *Ibn Battuta: Travels in Asia and Africa.* London: Darf Publications, 1983.

Hargraves, John D. *West Africa: The Former French States.* Englewood Cliffs, New Jersey: Prentice Hall, 1967.

Hughes, T. P. *A Dictionary of Islam.* London: W. H. Allen, 1885.

Hyslop, John. *Inca Road System.* New York: Academic Press, 1984.

July, Robert William. *A History of the African People.* New York: Scribner's, 1970.

Kinross, Lord. *The Ottoman Centuries: The Rise and Fall of the Turkish Empire.* London: Oxford University Press, 1977.

Lamb, Harold. *Genghis Khan.* Garden City, New York: Doubleday, 1927.

Liss, Peggy K. *Isabella the Queen: Her Life and Times.* New York: Walker, 1992.

Lofts, Norah. *Crown of Aloes.* Boston: G. K. Nell, 1974.

Lord, John. *Beacon Lights of History.* New York: Ford, Howard, and Hulbert, 1883.

Marcuse, Ludwig. *Soldiers of the Church, The Life of Ignatius Loyola.* New York: Simon & Schuster, 1939.

BIBLIOGRAPHY

Martin, Malachi. *The Jesuits: The Society of Jesus and the Betrayal of the Roman Catholic Church*. New York: Luder, 1987.

Matt, Leonard von. *Saint Ignatius of Loyola*. Translated by John Murray. Chicago: H. Regnary, 1956.

Maudslay, A. P., editor. *The Discovery and Conquest of Mexico 1517-1521*. London: George Routledge & Sons, 1928.

Mayer, Hans Eberhard. *The Crusades*. Suffolk: Oxford University Press, 1972.

McEwan, P. J. M. *Africa from Early Times to 1800*. London: Oxford University Press, 1968.

Murdock, George P. *Africa: Its Peoples and Their Culture History*. New York: McGraw-Hill, 1959.

Nicholson, R. A. *A Literary History of the Arabs*. Cambridge, England: Cambridge University Press, 1955.

Oliver, Roland, and J. D. Fage. *A Short History of Africa*. New York: New York University Press, 1965.

Olschki, Leonard. *Marco Polo's Asia*. Berkeley: University of California Press, 1960.

Ostrogorsky, George. *History of the Byzantine State*. New Brunswick, New Jersey: Rutgers University Press, 1957.

Painter, S. *A History of the Middle Ages, 1284-1500*. New York: Alfred Knopf, 1954.

Parringer, E. Geoffrey. *West African Religion*. London: Epworth Press, 1961.

Pears, Edwin. *The Fall of Constantinople, Being the Story of the Fourth Crusade*. London: Oxford University Press, 1985.

Pojman, Louis P., editor. *Introduction to Philosophy: Classical and Contemporary Readings*. Redwood City, California: Wadsworth, 1991.

Previte-Orton, C. W. *The Shorter Cambridge Medieval History*. Vol. 2. New York: Cambridge University Press, 1952.

Radin, Paul. *The Sources and Authenticity of the History of the Ancient Mexicans*. University of California Publications in American Archaeology and Ethnology, Vol. 17. Berkeley: University of California, 1920.

Rubin, Nancy. *Isabella of Castile: The First Renaissance Queen*. New York: St. Martin's Press, 1991.

Runciman, Steven. *A History of the Crusades*. Vol. 3. New York: Cambridge University Press, 1954.

Sherrard, Philip and the editors of Time-Life Books. *Byzantium*. New York: Time-Life, 1966.

Sherrard, Phillip. *Constantinople: Iconography of a Sacred City*. London: Oxford University Press, 1960.

Vaillant, George. *Aztecs of Mexico*. Garden City, New York: Doubleday & Co., 1941.

Van Dyke, Paul. *Ignatius Loyola, The Founder of the Jesuits*. New York: Scribner's, 1926

Wolfson, Freda. *Pageant of Ghana*. London: Oxford University Press, 1958.

Zuidema, Tom. *Inca Civilization in Cuzco*. Translated by Jean Jacques Decoster. Austin, Texas: University of Texas Press, 1990.

Index

Bold indicates entries and their page numbers; (ill.) indicates illustrations.

PROFILES IN WORLD HISTORY

Significant Events and the People
Who Shaped Them